Shine ONLINE

101

WAYS TO SHINE ON SOCIAL MEDIA

A Powerful Guide with Strategies to Help You
Maximize Your Presence Online
and Profit from Your Platform

Roshika 'Sunshine' West

PAPERBACK ISBN 978-1-7340574-7-8
EBOOK ISBN 978-1-7340574-2-3

Published by 20-West Entertainment & Media Company, LLC.

For Publisher Inquiries Contact: www.SunshineWest.Org/Contact or 20WestEntertainment@gmail.com

Signed Book Copy Request: www.LearnMediaToday.com and www.SunshineWest.org

Edits: Rolieria West, Julie Sykora and Morgan Blue
Book Design: Red Raven Book Design

Dedication

Intelligence is a community of practice, collectively moving towards the greater good of society. I dedicate my book to communities seeing the greater good.

I also dedicate this book to my nephew who brings a little light to my life with his bright smile and intelligent ways. The children are our future: Our influence influences them.

Lastly, this book is dedicated to family, their Sun Shines on me.

Table of Contents

About the Author
Sunshine West

Roshika 'Sunshine' West, is the educated and talented founder of the media production company 20-West Entertainment and Media Company and its media training branch Learn Media Today. West has a passion for digital communications and training others in her field to support them in their career or business endeavors. West's diverse background in media includes working with prestigious companies in various roles including public relations, film production, acting and TV broadcast on and off air in Atlanta, GA. However, gaining success started when West first embraced training in the diverse media landscape that Atlanta had to offer by gaining five media internships including working with Turner Broadcasting, WSB-TV and Tyler Perry Studios. Now, West leads her own media training company, Learn Media Today, in order to support other upcoming media professionals and businesses through providing online training and coaching in the areas of career development, social media, public relations and media production.

West welcomes you to pick her creative mind first via reading this book in which she provides numerous creative and proven strategies help you gain electric social media traction or "Shine Online". Secondly, West is available for you via online trainings, team meetings, and individual coaching. Please review www.sunshinewest.org or www.learnmediatoday.com for additional information on how she can help your brand shine using media.

Fun fact: West is a native of New Orleans, LA, an American art, music, and film mecca. West connected with the cultural influences of her hometown as a teen and became a visual artist. West's mantra from her birthplace is the classic New Orleans saying that provides inspiration: "Laissez Les Bon Temp Rouler", that is "Let the good times roll".

Introduction
What does it mean to Shine Online?

What does it mean to Shine Online? Shining online is the act of gaining both visual and analytic success while using social media to brand yourself online. It means you gain the followers you want and attention you need to garner the success you desire. Essentially, we all want to shine on social media for various reasons. If you are a business owner, you will likely want to stand out and present your brand in the best light. If you are a blogger with a personal brand, you will want to gain traction as an influencer. But how? Today, business owners, influencers, and bloggers are in a new type of rat race, it's a race against what some would consider creativity and content, but that's only half the battle. In addition to content creation, a great deal of social media success comes by implementing the best S.E.I.

- Strategic- Strategic, Emerging and Innovative Practices.

In our current digital media society, we are familiar with the fun aspects of connecting through social media. We frequently use online platforms for entertainment, social engagement, and collaborative communications, however, when it comes to best practices for business and branding, things tend to get complicated. When it concerns our social media, we ask ourselves, "So, how is my audience going to find me again?"

Although social media is meant to be user friendly, that doesn't instantly make every user a public relations guru with over 100k followers. That type of success not only takes time, but requires simple, but strategic skills. This text presents powerful strategies that most social media users do not apply, but that can positively impact followers, visits, and overall success Shining Online. You'll learn how to create a brand, create compelling content, and, last but not least, monetize your platform.

Whether you're a business owner, a blogger, a social media content manager or influencer, *101 Ways to Shine on Social Media* is your blueprint to reflect your best self and Shine Online by optimizing your social media platform, driving traffic and gaining influence. You'll benefit from my fourteen years of professional social media experience, five of which were engaged in research on contemporary media use while earning my Master's in Communications with a New Media Public Relations focus. My hope is that this book gives you the necessary tools to shine a bright light on your unique brand, grow your online influence and create and sustain success on social media.

It is your time to Shine Online. Utilize this book's 101 ways to grow your influence online to help you on your journey creating a brand. This book includes both strategic tactics as well as creative content ideas with the added bonus of monetization strategy. This is your go-to book when you just need an idea or are forming a social media plan for a special project. Enjoy your journey learning to Shining Online.

For more coaching strategies and helpful ideas, reach out to me on Instagram @LearnMediaToday.

Start Your Journey

Shining ONLINE

How to Use This Book

Firstly, I crafted this book of dynamic social media strategies for you--you the influencer and you business owner, with the purpose of helping your shine through providing strategic ideas and guidance for your social media to help you to build and evolve your brand for the better.

Shine Online: 101 Ways to Shine on Social Media is the ultimate guide for creation and promotion to make your social media pages shine and electrify your audience. While thinking of ways to build your brand, select the strategies provided that best align with your social media page to create a unique brand story. Start with your ideas and brand concept, then move to content ideas and specialized posts. For example, if you are a cupcake brand, start with the story of your brand, move to the look you want, then post the content that your brand needs most by using the engagement strategies in this book to help you.

To start, use the *Shine Online Social Media Strategy Building Method* below to create your brand story, design your concepts and create content.

Shine Online Strategy Building Method

What is my brand?

What am I hoping to offer my audience?

What do I hope that they, my audience, does?

What appearance do I want my social media to have to achieve my goals?

What media can I post that will inspire action?

Which shining strategies will I select today to move my brand forward?

How did my pages perform analytically (likes, etc.)?

Which strategies can I change or consistently adopt long term?

Please visit Instagram @LearnMediaToday and www.LearnMediaToday.com for more information on business strategies, live training and coaching or reach out directly at www.sunshinewest.org.

*For Special Worksheet to Help You Easily Implement These Strategies using: The B.I.G. Social Media Implementation Method, logon to www.LearnMediaToday.com

THE STRATEGY LIST AT GLANCE

CHAPTER I: My Journey Shining in Media & Business
CHAPTER II: Strategies for Powerful & Engaging Content
1. Provide Inspirational Content
2. Become Authentic
3. Start a Fresh Profile
4. Choose an Outstanding Username/Handle on Social Media
5. Display Your Passion & Talents
6. Share Your Purpose
7. Highlight Humanity & Community Service
8. Writing Stories Online/Micro Blog
9. Connect with Your Audience
10. Add Value to Your Community
11. Convert Followers Using Call to Action (CTA)
12. Collaborate Online
13. Implement Strategic Branding
14. Talk and Listen to Your Audience
15. Self-Presentation: Introduce Yourself
16. Stay On-Brand & "Feed" the Reason for Following
17. Boost Engagement: Add Interactive Elements
18. Consistent Posting: Post on a Regular Basis
19. Schedule Your Content Posts
20. Build Community Using "Hashtag Scrolls"
21. Take Social Off Social (Events)
22. Curate Your Page & Content
23. Be First
24. Co-Create a Social Media Page
25. Connect with Influencers or Become One
26. Be Creative
27. Follower Hack 1: Follower & Consumer Sharing
28. Follower Hack 2: VIP Follower Tagging
29. Follower Hack 3: Direct Contact
30. Spontaneity
31. Create a Style Guide for Consistency Across Platforms
32. Gain Loyal "Brand Followers"
33. Sunshine's Golden Rule: Be Good at Being Your Best Self

70.   Celebrating Who You Are
71.   Awareness
72.   Business: Create a Business Tribe
73.   Share Spiritual Knowledge & Content
74.   Showcase Special Skills
75.   Train Your Audience
76.   Special Day of Week Posts: Throwbacks, Flashbacks, etc.
77.   Team Collaboration & Groups
78.   Friendships
79.   Share Your Fab Lifestyle
80.   Repost & Share Content
81.   Video Snippets & Teasers
82.   Questions, Actions, & Polls
83.   Upcoming Events & Event Recaps
84.   Special Interest: Fashion, Modeling, Clothing & Accessories
85.   Special Interest: Health & Fitness
86.   Special Interest: Technology
87.   Special Interest: Beauty and Makeup Products
88.   Promotional Content Posts
89.   Entertainment Posts
90.   Artistic Posts
91.   Post About Your Business Services
92.   Behind the Scenes Photos (BTS)

CHAPTER VI: Strategic List for Making Money Online: Creating Profit from Your Platform
93.   Build Click Funnels $$$
94.   Blogs with Banners and Links
95.   Blogs as an Affiliate Influencer
96.   Selling Products Online, E-commerce
97.   Use Paid Advertisements & Sponsored Promotions
98.   Create Digital Education and Information Products
99.   Create a Podcast Series
100. Grow Your Following & Influence
101.   YouTube Video Ads: Sponsorship

Social Media Platforms that Shine

Top 10 Social Media Platforms for Brands in the U.S.

Social media is a challenge for many when it comes to things like how platforms work and how to build a brand, much less create a brand story. Help is here! I've provided a list of the "Top Ten Platforms in America for Brands," according buffer.com. These platforms are essential tools to advance your personal brand and shine on social media because they are proven magnets that attract users, and that's what you want to tap into. "There are 2.77 billion users across social media platforms, and they spend an average of 136 minutes on social media each day." (Elsbury, 2019). Use this list to help you find the ideal platform that works best to promote and illuminate your brand.

Top 10 Social Media Platforms to Boost Your Brand Online: (U.S.) (Buffer.com)

Instagram

Instagram is a photo sharing app that offers multiple ways to connect with your audience. The types of media you can share on Instagram include photo and video but are, they are only the tip of the iceberg in terms of what can be done to boost your brand. On Instagram, you can share not only photos, but videos via live feed, stories and Instagram TV (Scott, 2019). Content is king, so you can leverage Instagram to produce powerful content, tell your brand story, and amplify your social media page. Unique content and proven engagement strategies are discussed in this book. Instagram is a key resource for brands, and everyone is there. The numbers are astronomical: According to spoutsocial.com, in 2019, Instagram had 1-billion *active* monthly users (Barnhart, 2019). It's time to stop missing out and join the party by getting on the network! That's if you haven't already. Instagram is here for brands now more than ever, later in this book you find social media strategies to pump up your Instagram content, helping you to Shine Online.

Facebook

Facebook is the top social media sharing website and app with over 2 billion users logging on worldwide (Lua, 2019). Essentially, the number of active users = the number of unique people you can reach with your brand. Facebook is user friendly and business friendly but has been a source of controversy over the past few years due to privacy and policy issues. Despite those downfalls, it is still the #1 social media network that provides various ways to connect to users including messaging, posts, shares, groups and more. Business and brands will not come up short if they use Facebook tools well. We'll discuss how to effectively use Facebook tools like ads and business pages to attract users and make connections to stay in the mind of users and Shine Online.

Pinterest

Pinterest is a massive house of creative ideas shared by users that will help you with any project imaginable. For example, if you are hosting a baby shower and need some good ideas for decor- Pinterest boards provide loads of ideas to assist you in your creative efforts. But what does that have to do with you and your brand? Well, many bloggers and business owners are now using Pinterest to send users directly to their websites. To use Pinterest, create a board (using photos), and when a user clicks your visual to add it to their board or to "learn more," they are sent directly to your blog or website. Simply put, Pinterest is a giant hyperlink, so if you use it strategically, users will swarm your page and link to your blogs.

YouTube

YouTube is popular social media video posting and streaming platform with 1.9 billion active users per Buffer.com (Lua, 2019). We know YouTube as a video sharing platform full of entertainment recaps, news and influencers speaking to their audience. Each person has power in their own area of influence through their own expertise on YouTube. What the most viewer fails to realize is that half the YouTube influencers are not "super-gurus" or subject matter experts with doctorate degrees. They are simply people who had something to say and said it. The most successful YouTubers are consistently saying something relevant to their audience in an entertaining way. The book offers more strategies on using video and YouTube and monetizing your content in the last section.

Twitter (Twitterverse)

Tweet lately? Twitter is a microblogging site that boasts being the #12 social media network in terms of active users (Lua, 2019). Twitters likability has something with its real-time posting style, combined with the challenge of its 280-character limitation. So, the question is: If it's so popular how can it help me and my business shine and grow? Simply put, speak up. With Twitter you can speak your mind and post content that speaks to your audience's interests. Twitter also provides insights into what's at the top of mind of Twitter audiences and you can that information to make your posts relevant. This is key to keep your business glowing on Twitter, relevance and timing of current affairs posts.

*Politics are now huge Twitter. Twitter acts as a news knowledge base that is used as a resource by major news networks like CNN.

Snapchat

Whether or not you've personally used SnapChat, you've likely spotted a friend, family member or celebrity with a photo featuring the SnapChat filter's infamous flower crown on their heads. Snapchat can be a great deal of fun. But have you noticed branded filters for famous companies like Red Bull? They are on SnapChat nearly every day. Depending on your brand story, you can tap into the SnapChat market either as a primary or secondary tool, considering your current reach on other platforms. I do not recommend SnapChat as the only platform for a person or brand seeking to Shine Online for the first time. The best way to advance on SnapChat is to provide niche content or content people are crazy about and/or as a way to support your established brand as "bonus content."

Tumblr

Tumblr is a multi-media blogging site. Photographers and experts of self-expression and art can shine here. Are you willing to show your work? This might just be the place to gain a niche following. Tumblr is a useful site for a creative presentation of photo-based portfolios.

TikTok

TikTok currently hosts 500-million active users per buffer.com (Lua, 2019). TikTok is a social media platform that features short- form video similar to the website Vine. One of the interesting and attractive aspects of TikTok is that users are able to seemingly become professional video-makers due to the "special effects," like features that integrate graphic and digital editing into the videos (ABC News, 2018). Although, TikTok is based out of China, but is wildly popular among many markets including the U.S. The core demographic is age 10-19 followed by 20-29, with males being the number-one gender (Lua,2019). Businesses and brands can benefit from using the app though influencer marketing and partnerships. More information about partnerships is discussed in the section on monetization. The app is still growing in popularity, which allows influencers to be paid for live videos by users (ABC News, 2018). Understanding this platform, it's comedic and creative way of communicating to its young demographic will help you generate relatable content.

LinkedIn

LinkedIn is a career website in which users engage socially in support of their careers. Users create a resume and connect with other users in the career world. LinkedIn provides the opportunity to get in front of decision-makers and influencers to promote services and enhance careers.

LinkedIn is far more than a simple website for posting resumes. It has reached its Madonna phase, featuring blogs, multiple levels of connections, classes and professional groups. With a little research, you can identify a targeted audience to help grow your niche business. In addition, you can build a loyal following on LinkedIn by posting business-related blogs and photos to track your career success. The year 2020 and beyond continues to be the **era of authenticity** because professionals want to understand what you're about beyond the content in your online resume. Employers and others are looking for your entire digital picture because we all know social media can affect your career in a negative way. Provide that "social proof" of your career success through a complete and vibrant profile on LinkedIn with recommendations, blog posts and videos, which boosts authenticity in the eyes of others.

Blogs
Including WordPress

Blogs have a special place in my heart, because they are a great source of information. I currently have a blog and you can check mine out at **www.sunshinewest.org**. With website builders and sites like WordPress, blogs are not difficult to set up, but a successful blog requires a certain amount of dedication, consistency and compelling, relevant content. A successful blog combined with your shine on social networks is a powerful partnership that will catapult both mediums to success (Quicksprout.com, 2019). Your blog should be highly specialized in order reach your mainstream audience in order to build loyal supporters. Connecting it with other social media channels will depend on if they match. Does your Instagram content match what your long form content blog is about? If so, promoting your blog on your Instagram or other social media page will help your blog grow. Long form content blogs are great for presenting detailed information that will build strong support from those that read and visit your blog page (Patel, 2019).

Conclusion AboutPlatforms

As you can see, social media platforms are not one-size-fits-all, so it may take experimentation to understand what platforms reach your audience and best serve your brand. Learning to shine on social media means knowing your target audience and leveraging the most effective platform to optimize your content. Using social media platforms in a highly functional way is key. It's not just about looking good, it's about thoroughly knowing and reaching your audience.

You can shine on any platform and gain followers and conversion by using the following strategies that will show you how to grow and Shine Online.

Chapter 1

My Journey Shining in Media and Business

I started my first business when I was just a child at seven years old. I grabbed old school empty green strawberry baskets, some old stuff from around the house (I guessed nobody wanted), I made some flyers and gave them to the neighbors. I had my first ever yard sale. Thus, I have always had a passion for business as I come from a family of business owners. Yet, as you can guess, my seven- year-old marketing strategy is no longer the best way to market a business, not even a yard sale.

If I were a child business owner today, I'd have a Facebook and Instagram page for my business, and I'd blog about my life as a business owner and share important dates for sales. This is because we now live in "the era of digital influence" where brands grow online.

When I began my career in media as a young adult and college student in Atlanta, attending Georgia State University, I learned everything about media the old way. I learned about traditional media channels like ground telecommunications, wires, live satellite broadcast and the one thing all communicators desire to do; to get your point across. However, one thing was missing from my textbooks at the time. Facebook had just emerged among students and I was curious about it. Blogs were still a bit of a mystery; there were three whole pages about it in my telecommunications book.

Without any reservation I began to learn media by first stepping in front of the camera and acting in feature films, including a Tyler Perry movie. Next, I worked at four media internships behind the scenes including working in broadcast news, cable TV at Turner Broadcasting System, magazine reporting and a short stint in radio promotions to get the ball rolling. Communications in my former jobs were initially all about writing and branding in more of a one-directional communication to convince your audience to love your brand. Flash forward to present day, media marketing has evolved and is now about social media listening, collaborating and influencing.

My diverse background in public relations, new media, film, television, art, policy and media training has really rounded out my expertise in creative media and I understand the ins and outs of running and marketing a business. In this guide, I share the keys to branding online and engaging an audience through social media. I've been around long enough to witness not only social media strategies change over time, but also the way social media is in constant flux as it adjusts to users' needs. Even social media marketers have to continuously learn strategies that will keep the brands they manage on top of the social media food chain. And in this space, what has emerged is something called the "voice of influence" (VOI). I'll show you how to create your own shine by adding value to your brand through your own VOI."

We are now living in the "era of influence" in which we can take charge of our brand in ways we could not previously. The era of influence is right now, when online mediated self-expression and expertise results in a high level of social connection, influence, leads and business outputs. Simply put, influence acts as a marketing tool where the chief tool at work is the influencer or online communicator/social media page owner. The influencer or creator builds a "tribe," loyal followers who are so invested in the creator's brand and content, that members of this tribe will purchase just about anything. This is only achieved because the influencer has consistently posted on-brand content that the tribe is excited about. So, why is this so important to understand? Just think about how in just a few short years, Kylie Jenner's Instagram made the cover of *Forbes* titled "Billion-Dollar Baby" due to her mass promotion of beauty products. Understanding how to stand out and influence online is essential for both new brands seeking to inspire customers as well as individuals desiring to elevate themselves by becoming influencers to profit online.

However, attaining a significant following sounds easier than it is, and that's why you're here! Here's the thing: Not all "likes" are created equal. You may wonder why two individuals garner 100 likes per post, but one of them results in very little engagement.

Sometimes it simply comes down that individual having an online presence for longer than the other. Most of the time and more importantly, it has to do with how your content is received by your audience. What feelings are evoked when they land on your page? Are they learning something? Are you offering something they need? Are you inspiring them or intimidating them by information overload?

If all of this is overwhelming at the moment, no worries, that's what I'm here for! I'll show you how a *strategic approach* with an authentic spin will lead to increased influence and Shine Online. I've provided both known and emerging strategies to impact your audience and yield outputs.

To start, you can't grow your brand or generate business leads without an online audience. I'll show you how to target, grow and influence your desired audience by speaking to them directly, and by understanding what they actually think via online engagement methods.

Your journey in the new era of influence starts now. It starts by understanding your brand, then platforms, and finally strategies that work. A few things to keep in mind as you read through *101 Ways to Shine Online:* While reviewing strategies for social media influence and monetization think about: 1.) How to align your brand with the strategies that make sense for your brand. 2.) Make sure you jot down notes about technical strategies speak to you. and 3.) Note creative ideas that you'd like to implement on social media while you're reading. If you'd like more discussion, follow me or spark up a conversation @LearnMediaToday.

So, it begins, *your* time to influence and to Shine Online starts now!

The Strategic List for Shining Online: Social Media Strategies for Success

Instagram: @ShineOnline.Book
#ShineOnlineBook2020

Chapter 2

Strategies for Powerful
& Engaging Content

In the world of social media, it is not enough to simply have content or post something. Your content should illuminate, be powerful and engaging. The goal should be to Shine Online using content that elicits specific engagement such as follows, likes, shares, messages and comments. This starts by understanding your brand and audience. Next, start reaching your audience by employing the following shining social media strategies to create powerful and engaging content. Remember, understanding how to create engaging content is important because more engagement you get, the more your loyalty grows. As loyalty builds, so will your potential to build a profitable brand through social media.

1
Provide Inspirational Content
#SunshineInspo

Shining online can easily be misconstrued as a self-serving way to show off on social media; however, fame and influence are obtained in the exact opposite way. Being in service of others via your online content will surely make you shine in a positive light. One way to serve others is to inspire them by a personal story, a famous quote, an original quote, or a photo. The key is to reach the audience's emotions while being on-brand. Simply posting a quote or a photo without purpose will not create the loyal following you want.

Always present moving, emotionally fueled content wrapped in the brand you're building to create inspirational posts that allow you to Shine Online because they give your audience a chance to get to know you by understanding your personality and what you really care about. This builds loyalty to your brand, which in turn, builds consumer confidence.

For example, take a profile for a career coach. The coach's objective is to get as many clients as possible by creating posts about persistence, hard work, and success with the underlying message that success can be yours if you hire me as your coach. This content not only seeks to inspire emotionally, but also moves the audience to action to "like," "connect," and/or "follow."

In order to shine through inspiration, think of something that your core audience is hungry to hear. Using widely known quotes and media is effective to a point. Yet, it often helps when you create your own quotes and inspired communications because your unique voice will surface from original content and your followers will start to recognize and seek it out.

Inspirational posts can be posted on the following platforms: Instagram, Facebook, Twitter, Pinterest, Blogs, LinkedIn and more. If you can say it, there is a way to post it.

2
Become Authentic

What does it mean to speak through your almighty "authentic voice?" Well, it is not almighty because it's your voice, your brand, and your authentic style of communicating. It is also clearly communicating your values, ethics, and background. It is speaking to your audience in a relatable way, like chatting with a friend where your voice and brand feel familiar and comfortable. Your brand messages feel welcoming and not forced. You are engaging in human relations.

Some influencers are great at connecting authentically by storytelling and superior writing, but some are not as successful. To be successful at this you must remember that people viewing your profile (followers or not) desire to make decisions themselves. They make decisions by reviewing your content. The more authentic it is, the more likely they are to become fans and buy into following your profile. Without authenticity--- there will be some disconnect with your audience. While some people might check out your website, they won't trust you until they know more and can hear or see your authentic voice on your profile. Shine through using your unique voice via the relatable media you post.

Bright Idea: To connect with your authentic voice review what matters to you and your brand most. Ask yourself: How can I convey what matters to me or my brand? What are my daily challenges? How can I show my audience my position without sounding like a salesman?

3
Start a Fresh Profile

Starting fresh means either cleaning up your profile or getting a new one. For example, you can deactivate your Facebook account from 2004, when you were a college student with questionable friends and activities to match. You are becoming a new person online, your best self, so you need to renew your profile by clearing old clutter: photos, friends, videos, and old notes. Take on new skin by rebranding your social media profile to reflect the brand that you are seeking to project to your followers. Of course, the world was not built in a day, so as you continue to develop your brand, you will discover new ways to construct your social profiles and keep it fresh and shining. If you're introducing a new brand, cleanse your old-branded media and create your new profile with a re-branded media campaign. You will find that new brand attracts your core audience and collaborative brands.

4

Choose an Outstanding Username/Handle on Social Media

Good usernames/social media handles pull people into your profile via social media algorithms and also help you build community.

Currently, Instagram uses an algorithm system that identifies your *username* in association with your ranking on social media. This means that if you are a CEO, writer, or graphic designer, use a username on Instagram that explains your brand, because Instagram identifies users interested in who you are and displays your profile to more of those interested users.

Ranking in this way is helpful because users that have similar interests to yours or who are interested directly in you, are more inclined to like your posts and visit your profile. Interest is the key to shining online. When you create your profile, take the time to be crystal-clear about who you are and what you do, and you will attract exactly those in your industry who need what you are offering. Whether you are an accountant, a fashion influencer, or a chef, you will Shine Online through having a social media handle and description on your social media pages that is in-line with what you do and what you have to offer.

5
Display Your Passion & Talents

What is passion when it comes to social media? Passion on social media simply means displaying what you really care about and/or what you love to do and showing it out loud. So, what does that mean if, say, you love cooking, drawing, or singing? You can shine by not only displaying your work, but also telling people what your passion means to you. Even if your passion is teaching or technology, that counts too! It's all in how you present it.

The odds are that other people who also share your passion will be willing to:

- Follow you

- Become your fan

- Share valuable content you post (exposing you to new followers)

Shining through your passion is as simple as consistently showing off what you love and sharing It wIth the world. Those that appreciate it will let you know by compliments, likes, and following you. If you are a professional in the area that you are passionate about, posting about it can help you grow in popularity and gain more followers and potential customers if your passion is also a business. **Shine Online by finding creative ways to display your talents and connect with your audience through allowing them to compliment you, while you show your gratitude via listening and replying.**

#Talented

Sunshine West shows her talent for hosting and entertainment while shooting a media production.

6
Share Your Purpose

Sometimes telling people your purpose is all you need to start growing. You could tell a compelling story of why you have a certain profile, brand or business. What's your story? For example, you sell real estate to get people into homes because you were homeless once and you want to help people find their perfect home. This is a story worth telling. Use video, storytelling captions or photos or a combination to shine a light on who you are, what makes you tick, what motivates you and what you have to offer. This, in turn, will yield more trust from your online audience, making them loyal fans of your brand.

7
Highlight Humanity & Community Service

Highlighting your passion for humanity through community service, fundraisers and informative posts about them are all ways to Shine Online while also supporting your cause. Showing your online audience that you care about something other than followers and likes will show people that you are not just about what you can get, but what you can give. This is another way of building trust with your audience. Allowing your passion for humanity to shine through posting about it online and connecting with online communities and individuals with a similar passion will draw followers that believe in and admire what you are doing. To engage your audience about your support for a cause, let your audience know why that cause is important to you and your engagement in that cause.

8

Writing Stories Online/ Micro Blog

Writing stories on social media is also called microblogging. The longer that your followers spend reading a post on Instagram, the more the Instagram algorithm works in your favor. Why? Because the app is concerned with engagement. Once the app notices that followers like or are engaged in your post for a while, they will display it more in the Instagram feed.

This is something to think about: I was afraid to write lengthy posts because I thought that people would shy away from spending time to read it. The key is to pair your compelling story text with an equally compelling photo or visual. The advantage of a written post leaves an impression on the viewers because it feels like reading a letter or a blog versus just looking at a plain or superficial photo.

To shine using microblogging be sure that your blogs are on brand and create engagement. You can review the level of engagement of your microblog via responses on social media including viewership, likes and increased followers. Refer to strategies (1, 2, 6, 10 and 11 for more help on creating engaging content you can include in your microblog.)

MicroBlog

9
Connect with Your Audience:

Connecting on social media sounds simple enough, but it is often complex in practice. You need to know your audience and their interests. There are two forms of connecting: literal and figurative. Literal connection occurs when you actively taken action to relate with a profile by communicating online like commenting or doing the unthinkable- following someone or liking their post in return.

Figurative connection is connecting with what your audience wants. In order to "connect," ask yourself what is your brand and why are people interested? Nailing down your main point of interest will result in focused posts that connect with your audience. Ask yourself, "What would I want to know?" "Are my posts random or relatable?" And then post the most relevant photos and captions that relate to your audience's interests and watch the connections evolve. Connections lead to growth and growth leads to shining on social media to build your brand.

10
Add Value to Your Community

Adding value on social media means providing useful content to your audience, such as teaching or demonstrating something to your audience, or simply inspiring them in some way. Why is valuable content essential to attract viewers to Shine Online? Adding value creates a genuine reason for someone to return to your page, become your fan and also buy something from you either immediately or down the line.

Just to be clear, the valuable content I'm referring to does not have to be an entire book or body of work. You'll provide value through content such as a short video talking about something you are an expert at or a brief infographic post. Posting content like this builds interest, helps you shine as an expert or motivator and keeps the audience wanting more.

Value posts can also be entertaining. For example, make-up artists who teaches how to apply make-up via videos may have background music playing or lively commentary that he or she presents that makes the valuable content fun to view.

Bright Ideas: Social Media Posts that Add Value.

- Infographics
- Helpful Lists
- Photos with value comments (micro blog)
- Inspirational Videos
- Informative Videos

11
Convert Followers Using Call to Action (CTA)

CTA = Asking for what you want, catching subscribers while they're in a "your profile" type of mood.

A call to action (CTA) social media post inspires a specific action. A call to action is a verbal, text or graphic post that tells the audience to do something or "take action" for an intended purpose. Why is this important? In marketing, the call to action is like *almost* reaching the finish line because it is the point after promotion and marketing where people are asked to do something that will benefit the brand. This could be text that prompts the audience to follow you, like your post, register for a course, etc.

The call to action text is a special promotion tool and is written and executed strategically. You should use CTA for quick and direct actions (Mulvey, 2018). For example, we have all seen posts stating, "If you agree, like this post." Whether or not a user agrees, she might like the post simply because it asks her to do so. There might also be a special incentive for taking action, like registering with a website for a free guide. However, the best call to action posts gain results by compelling or inspiring your audience in some way.

Example CTA Post 1: You have cupcake baking brand. You display a photo full of your baked goods and you ask the audience to go an order now before they are all out.

Example CTA Post 2: You provide five reasons that your current customers come back to buy your baked goods along with mouthwatering photos of your luscious cupcakes at baked-goods events and describe customers' reactions. Finally, you ask them to try your cupcakes for themselves at a discounted rate on the date of the post. Your audience is likely to respond to the CTA due to the added incentive from your compelling content.

Simple Call to Action Formula:

- Detailed Photo > Caption describing value of your product > Provide success story > State call to action > Provide easy access to the action
- Video introduce yourself> Talk about your service > Highlight your service's success> Voice your call to action at least two times with incentive > Provide easy access to action.

Bright Ideas: The promotional written or spoken structure of a call to action (CTA) posts should flow like this:

1. Start with promotional information (a story)

2. Note the previous success gained by others (results)

3. Note how it can benefit them (potential customer or follower)

4. Then pitch the call to action by stating what they have to do to get that result. (CTA = desired outcome)

This is a fairly simple CTA writing structure that you can apply to your brand. If you master this method along with an easy way for people to take action, you will generate leads through shining CTA content.

#CTA

12
Collaborate Online

Collaborating is one of the most powerful things you can do to shine on social media because it helps you to engage online and broaden your audience. Online collaboration can result in offline customers; however, mobilizing online through collaboration is an essential step that often comes before offline engagement. Collaboration involves creating a community and consistently communicating with them. The goal is to grow your audience and to mobilize them for a specific purpose like a special event.

For example, if you are a blogger and you can connect regularly with other bloggers via Instagram comments and posts. You and your fellow bloggers can collaborate via commenting and liking posts on each other's profiles. Later, collaborate with the bloggers for a special event, which brings you both additional followers. For example, host a Facebook Live event with another of blogger or expert to discuss their area of expertise in connection with yours.

Bright Ideas: 7 Keys to Collaborating on Social Media:

1. Find your community and follow them.

2. Find those with complementary interests so that you can collaborate

3. Build or join a community of like-branded people where you all comment and like each other's content.

4. Utilize multi-media platforms like Facebook Live, Instagram Live, and YouTube Live to host collaborative online meetings with your audience. The resulting combined followings with help you both shine on social media.

5. Create more moments to share online by taking your newfound collaborators from social media to in-person events in your local community.

6. Share your experiences and photos of what others post about you #Repost.

7. If you need collaboration, just ask. You have an equal chance of getting rejected as you do obtaining a much-needed collaboration.

13
Implement Strategic Branding

Aesthetic feeds are increasingly popular. They give your page a look and feel with which your audience can identify.

Branding is the concept behind your business or your personal representation. Having a well-known, easy to recognize brand on social media will allow your audience to recognize you across different platforms. Good branding and effective promotion happens when your overall thought concept is support visually.

Branding can be implemented via many visual methods including a logo design, specific color schemes, or graphic styles unique to your brand. Other ways of branding your company include creating specific services or even a slogan. Your social media brand and look should match all of your brand's guidelines. For example, Pepsi is branded with the colors red, white and blue (combined various ways throughout the years), and Pepsi's social media website is composed of the same color scheme, with lots of red, white and blue. To support their brand, Pepsi's website also parades happy people having a great time with Pepsi in-hand. That evokes positive feelings about the Pepsi brand in the minds of their social media followers, thereby supporting their brand using a highly relatable branding tactic.

Clearly, Pepsi is a mega brand and no one is expecting that level of branding from small business owners because most will not to have multiple marketing teams to create and maintain their social media branding. However, if you follow a few simple guidelines, you can create a solid brand that people admire, go to and recognize. Here a few strategic branding guidelines to help you shine on social media and be remembered in the minds of your followers and online visitors.

Bright Ideas: How to Start Branding Online

- Decide on a theme that is in line with your company's goals and values.

- Pick a color scheme and design style.

- Get a logo that matches your color scheme.

- Use posts designed to match that color scheme/brand concept.

- Ensure your messages remain on-brand by reviewing how your audience perceives them.

- Keep it fresh by occasionally re-branding (switch it up a bit & shine!)

This is not an all-inclusive list of branding techniques or guidelines, but these are essential to optimize your brand online. A well-executed brand that people recognize and relate to will help you get the social media shine and build the momentum you desire.

For more information and assistance building your brand see the section titled Strategy Guide: The Shine Online Strategy Building Method or contact me at www.learnmediatoday.com and direct on www.Instagram.com/LearnMediaToday.

14
Talk and Listen to Your Audience

Talking and listening to your audience means starting the conversation to engage with your online audience and moderating it (Kerpen, Rosenbluth, & Riedinger, 2015). When people comment on your posts, feel free to comment back with response that show you are interested in what they have to say. Not only are you engaging your audience in this way, but it's a great opportunity to respond with gratitude or reply to audience questions to keep the conversation going. Talking to the audience is also done through videos and live stories. You can respond via video to burning questions that your audience has wanted to know or provide them with information they have asked for in your comments or direct messages.

Listening to audience and replying to comments are always helpful when wanting to shine on social media because your audience and followers develop more trust in you when you talk to them directly. Listening to your audience can also improve your brand because you will understand what your audience enjoys most by what they respond to. Overtime, you can improve your brand and Shine Online, through listening.

#Listen

15
Self-Presentation: Introduce Yourself

Self-presentation is when you introduce yourself online to a new audience. This can be done via video, a slide show or a single photo with comments. The purpose of introducing yourself to your audience is to gain their trust and interest by letting them know more about you. For example, if you are teaching a Photoshop course, you might post a video of yourself speaking about your background in photography, how you acquired skills and discovered a passion for Photoshop. You've just created credibility and trust, which might mean the difference between a potential follower or customer and a lost one. It presents you in a personable way and lets your audience know why you are an authority.

16
Stay On-Brand & "Feed" the Reason for Following

Sometimes a random post will get you unfollowed.

To "feed the reason" for following is a strategy that goes along with consistency, content curation and branding. If you are, for example, a food-based blog and people expect food videos, photos and blog posts and suddenly, you post a random video of you skiing or multiple posts about your break-up, you will alienate followers. Yes, we are all human, and many Internet users seek out the element of surprise, but if your posts get too random, expect to be unfollowed by some users.

Users want to understand who they are following. There will be times when you have a random thought or are suffering in some way, just pause and think: "Should I be posting this online? Is this relevant to my brand?" There's a fine line between coming across as overly manufactured and inauthentic and oversharing personal matters just for the sake of having something to say. Be careful. This is why it's so important to know your audience. So, go ahead and post your engagement, vacation and "outfit of the day", using the hashtag made popular by reality star, Stassi Schroeder, (#OOTD), but don't be so quick to post negative memes or something so gross you that lose followers. Feed the reason for following your brand with thoughtful, on-brand, posts and you will Shine Online.

17

Boost Engagement: Add Interactive Elements

Connecting, collaborating and commenting. If people engage with you, you should engage with them back for your brand. Social engagement is the thread that weaves though many of the tenants in this guide. Engagement means being active in your social media online community, including joining online groups, commenting, sharing, liking, and creating content for your community. Engagement is a broad term that can be broken down into essential components. The list below covers ways to engage online, but it is not all-inclusive because new social media networks and engagement modes are ever emerging. Currently, emerging engagement methods include "live communications" and live feed story sharing.

Bright Ideas: Ways to Be Engaged Online

1. Create content with links.

2. Comment back on posts.

3. Like posts on others' social media.

4. Respond online.

5. Join online groups.

6. Share other users' posts online (example- Twitter reposts).

7. Add quizzes and interactive elements to your posts or stories on Facebook or Instagram.

18

Consistent Posting: Post on a Regular Basis

Posting consistently on your social media is another key to shining online because it allows you to build a faithful following while also maintaining your brand. And what is consistency? Every week? Month? Day? It depends. What are your goals and, more importantly, what have you communicated to your audience that you will do? If you have told your audience that you will post twice weekly or every Monday, do so. If you have created no expectations, but would like to create consistency, start doing so by pre-creating posts or integrating a scheduling system or service to achieve the consistency your audience expects and wants.

The benefits of consistency are not just for the audience, but also for you. You will be building your brand and a more faithful following that believes in your content. If you believe in it enough to post, your audience will begin to believe that you are authentic.

Posting consistently and remaining authentic can be a challenge. Remember to always be true to your brand. Experiment with what you followers like and appreciate, which will make the process of posting consistently easier over time. Your brand will reach its full potential through consistent authentic posts that become exciting but familiar potential customers.

Bottom line: If you want to grow, post consistently.

19

Schedule Your Content Posts

Scheduling your social media posts is helpful to maintain a business or influencer site because you always have content and there's a flow and rhythm even while you are not personally posting. Scheduling can be accomplished through websites like Buffer.com, which provides scheduled social media content posting services. Keep in mind that the scheduling of prepared posts should not be considered as unauthentic, but rather a preparation of what you have carefully created, reviewed and/or discovered was worthy to post. Evaluate your scheduled content to make sure it's staying on-brand through time. Is the information timely for what your followers expect? While scheduling posts gives you the freedom to *not* be on social media creating posts all the time, you should use that time to focus on analytics and creating great content. Scheduled content also will help you shine by providing consistency for your followers.

20
Build Community Using "Hashtag Scrolls"

One interesting way to build community is to scroll through hashtags. Hashtags, also known as trending topics, are now the new built-in powerhouse of social media. On Instagram, a user can now follow a hashtag topic like #LearnMediaToday without being attached to a specific user. Why? Even Instagram has discovered that there are successful social media gurus and mega influencers online that spend hours searching for and growing their audience using what I call, "hashtag scrolls," which is finding a topic by scrolling through hashtags to determine what your audience or industry is interested in. Then, you can begin to engage with like- minded people in a "sub-folder" with just those people, interested in that hashtag. Now, no doubt there will be some random posts using certain hashtags just to get attention, however the majority will lead you to your like-minded tribe. Your tribe helps you to shine by building a community. Once, you find genuine supporters who are interested in what you have to offer, you are on your way to not just shining online but becoming an influencer. Utilize hashtag scrolls to spike engagement and find your community. You may be surprised by the content you find and what you learn about how others promote topics associated with your brand.

Hashtag Scroll

21

Take Social Off Social (Events)

Move the audience to a purchase, event or better.

Whether one considers social media good or bad, one thing is certain, social media connects us. For brands who can, it is a good idea to take your online brand offline for special events. This is true community building because the purposes for gathering are limitless. However, *that* purpose must be well supported online via well-advertised posts and high awareness online. Shining to your new group after an event will boost your brand because word of mouth about experiences spreads fast on social media due to photo sharing and tagging. Thus, if your followers have a great time or gain something from your event, they will look forward to the next offline event for your brand.

To create posts about offline events, ensure that all of the offline event information is available and easy to find on your social media posts. Share posts about the event or advertise it for increased success. You can also use built-in interest groups like those on Facebook to find niche audiences quickly.

22

Curate Your Page & Content

Curating content on your social media page involves design concepts with a deep meaning. In general, curating social media pages means creating a design and brand concept that balances your social media page and creates an overall "feel." Before the age of 12, I painted over 50 works of art, so I am blessed with artistic skills. I now apply that skill and design nearly all of my original social media posts, so I'll share a little bit about curation and design.

Curation is the balance of aesthetics or visual elements involved in a design. Is your social media page a design? Well, for many it is. Have you ever noticed that on Instagram because there are three block columns, some brands or influencers will post three photos with a similar theme? Or they will post a photo, a quote graphic and then another photo, thereby creating balance on the curated Instagram line. To put it simply, curating is the concept behind your brand.

The deeper meaning is that the colors, styles or posting pattern you display should be unique and meaningful to your brand. On Instagram, you can easily become an artist. Say you are an Army Veteran. You would use hunter green and various hues of green because they are Army colors and symbolize your service. You want to incorporate your military service with your services as a photographer. That is a form of curation with purpose. Of course, the purpose could be simply because a color or style pattern looks good, but it is up to you. The point is to think of a concept and stick to it by understanding how you want your page to look to a new visitor. Sometimes people are fascinated by your consistent use of colors, filters or lighting and join your following to see more.

Curating doesn't just include your page's overall look to new viewers, but also includes what specific content you post, on what day, and why. If you are struggling, the question to ask about a post or a photo is, "How does this fit into my brand?" Answer your own question with content that fits and appears how you want your brand to appear.

Bright Ideas: Ways to Curate Content

- Think of a theme (using colors or ideas).
- Consistently use that theme.
- Use post patterns (photo and graphic balance, see example).
- Select filters that will appear often in your photos.

23

Be First

One great way to shine on social media is to sign up early for new social media platforms in order to reserve your desired brand name because there are professionals who buy website domains that are well-known names on social media in hopes of either gaining attention or selling the domains. With social media, this is not a huge issue as people are now altering their social media handles and usernames to anything. However, if you desire consistency across platforms, securing those same usernames across your main platforms is a must for long-term branding success on social media.

24

Co-Create a Social Media Page

Creating a blog or Instagram page with a partner can be fun   as well has help you shine on social media. This could be dating partners, married partners or blogging partners. If you are creating content and ideas together, not only is it double the fun, but also double the ideas and strategy. Keep in mind, when or if you split, know you will need to start fresh on a new brand. Partner brands do well, especially for social media that focuses on experiences or businesses. How much you will shine depends on the interest and value generated from your partnership.

25

Connect with Influencers or Become One

Social media influencing will help you get to the next level. You can collaborate with a larger influencer or you can become one through creating your own expert content. According to author of Influencer, Brittany Hennessey, there are two types of influencers: content creators and life casters (Hennessey, 2018). Content creators create expert or engaging content that social media users gain value from. Life casters have interesting lives and social media users love peeking on their profiles to follow their lifestyle or adventures. For this, book, Shine Online, we'll focus on how connecting with content creator influencers can help your brand to grow (Hennessey, 2018).

Collaborating with influencers allows you to connect with their larger following and allow you to gain exposure for your brand's offerings. Often, an agreement to pay the influencer or barter for their services is a worthy exchange for exposure to their audience. For example, imagine that you have a new make-up line and a smaller following on social media, now think of a famous make- up artist with 100,000 followers in social real estate using products from your make-up line on social media as a way of advertising your product. Thus, connecting or partnering with the influencer can provide reach to your brand that you otherwise would not have. In addition, the influencer that you select should have influence in the industry that connects well with your brand. For example, a healthy food product can be promoted well by a fitness influencer. Building connections with an influencer will require research and direct partnership with that online influencer or selection from an influencer agency.

If you are the influencer looking to build a profitable brand, you can also promote your own products frequently and show your audience the quality of your product. Instructing your followers and guiding them along increases your impact as an influencer because you become the go-to person for your audience in your space. Becoming an influencer on YouTube and Instagram is becoming increasingly popular as the apps grow in popularity. To start shining as an influencer, select a platform you will primarily use and idea in which you are an expert and start creating content. Overtime, if your content is valuable, your influence will grow. Use content strategies from this book to help guide your path Shining Online as an influencer.

26
Be Creative

Thought Bubble: Unique content helps you create a brand and push it forward. Use creative ideas of other brands or create your own. Creating your own unique ideas means your social media will have its own shining look, brand and content like no one else.

Utilizing the infinite world of creativity is one way to shine on social media. Creativity is not limited to special artists but can be honed by an analytical thinker as well. You just have to be willing to try an idea not previously tried or tweak something in   a way that's never been tried before. That's being creative. What signature hashtag can you create for your special event? (For example, #CupCakeDay2020) What way can colors and visuals be used on your profile that will attract the eye and bring people to you? What do you want to say on Instagram or Facebook stories that would delight viewers and maintain their interest? Be creative and original by creating your own quotes, graphics or ideas. Your audience will appreciate seeing some creativity. For my own brand, once I began creating my own quotes and graphics, my social media spiked because new profile viewers and current followers were seeing something on my profile that they couldn't find elsewhere. Shine Online via coming up with creative ideas and testing them on your social media page.

27

Follower Hack 1:
Follower & Consumer Sharing

What does it take to really blow up your brand, to make it shine in the eyes of people who've never heard of you? It takes a loyal follower community for others to take notice. One of the top follower hacks is brand follower and consumer sharing. Follower and consumer sharing occur when users of your brand's product or service share your product on their own social media sites. Their shares act as endorsements for you, called social proof. Social proof means you're respected and trusted and will catapult lead generation.

Why is this a hack? And does it really work? Yes. It is one of the

top ways to build a brand from the ground up without paying for advertisements. Another way to boost your brand is to pay affiliates, which is paying someone to post your product/service (I'll cover that later). You can leverage the community you build to be of service to you by asking them to share something specific. Again, sharing opens new doors by exposing you to their followers and their followers' followers. This follower hack can help you shine and be trusted by new users online. Remember that social media "users" are also people, and people tend to gravitate towards those trusted by others, upholding the age-old principle, "It's not what you know but who you know".

To Shine Online to new users, utilize follower shares and consumer shares. Consumer shares are when people share your products online and follower shares consists of any follower sharing activity that promotes your brand. The best way to utilize this sharing strategy is to use a call to action. You can do this by saying, "If you liked my shades, share with your friends and receive a discount on your next order." Or "If you like my cooking video, share for a chance to win a custom spoon designed by me!" Strategies to shine are limitless, it just takes a little creativity and caring for your followers as you want them to evangelize your brand. To sum it up, offer something solid for your followers to share and their word of mouth, good karma and shares will brighten your Shine Online.

28

Follower Hack 2: VIP Follower Tagging

Take the last 20 people that liked your new book announcement, the last 50 people that liked your photo or the seven people that *loved* your photo enough to comment on it. When you have important posts, you can address these users by tagging them specifically to those announcements or calls to action. Calls to action can include a product announcement, a special event or a community initiative. How does this change your follower growth activity? This strategy is two-pronged. The first part deals with exposure. You gain exposure to your tagged followers' followers (if others can see their tagged posts). The second part is that those tagged feel as though they are gaining incentives for being associated with you online because tagging for a specific reason (to inform or offer) is a form of direct contact. Getting a free offer, announcement or information due to direct contact will make your followers feel they are important and appreciated. You'll gain their loyalty, support and new followers through the wonderful comments by your loyal fans on your popular post. Shine through being loyal to your followers when you have something important to say and say it directly by tagging your most engaged followers to special posts.

29

Follower Hack 3: Direct Contact

Direct contact is one of the more interesting strategies for boosting your brand because it encourages the follower loyalty needed to sustain your brand. Direct contact is when you directly contact your followers to, for example, thank them for a purchase or for following them, or maybe even to follow up on a service. This a kind of social media cold calling. It is the direct touch that tells people you appreciate them or shows your brand is all about excellent service and relationships.

Building loyalty this way reduces follower turnover. Oftentimes, social media users hit a plateau where they can't seem to get new followers, despite staying consistently on-brand. Perhaps new followers are not the issue, it may be a combination of gaining new followers and suffering follower turnover or unfollowing that has you in a snag. To reverse this, speak to your audience by thanking those that like or comment on your posts. Answer their questions and send a personalized message to your most faithful followers. They already love your shine, but they will become bigger fans and support buy-in to your engaged brand.

30.
Spontaneity

Is your social media profile too perfect or predictable? Don't be so curated that you lose your sense of spontaneity and/or your content becomes one-dimensional. People want to know the person behind the business and what that person or brand specifically brings. One example of spontaneous social media occurs when social media users participate in challenges that make their social media go viral. The perception is that person is audacious or talented enough to participate in this challenge and that generates interest. Have you ever won an award or received a special honor? People love that stuff, yet many users stick to such a high level of planned content that boxes them in, so they never think outside of the box. If you are an influencer, shine through being spontaneous on social media by thinking of something you haven't been doing for the last five weeks and going for it. For example, if you are a finance coach, instead of posting solely about financial literacy, post about how you ran up credit card debt when you were a college student and how you resolved it. Your audience will appreciate you shaking things up and they will appreciate knowing the real you, the one they can connect to. Spontaneous or unexpected posts should also be on -brand and not break the connection that you have with your followers but make it stronger through them viewing interesting content.

31
Create a Style Guide for Consistency Across Platforms

No matter how many platforms your company uses, it's important to have consistency throughout them all. It takes valuable time for companies to build a brand on social media and using a style guide helps you send a unified message through all the content and platforms that represent your brand. Forbes.com says, "...use colorful and informative infographics." This is to get as many "likes" and "shares" as possible because social network algorithms will be more favorable and rank you higher in the feed as your engagement grows. My personal experience is that understanding your brand's style and creating some guidelines makes the process of branding easier overtime because you will not be constantly searching for outstanding new styles and fonts for brand posts. Although having some unique posts are important, a style guide will to keep your brand ideas on track. Style guides also help brands to manage their social media using multiple people or teams because with a style guide, any team member can create a post that is consistent with the styles and standards of your brand. This works well for growing and larger businesses that have multiple social media managers.

#StyleGuide

32

Gain Loyal "Brand Followers":

A brand follower is a fan who is a diehard to the end. They give total loyalty a new meaning and always support your endeavors. The great thing about brand followers is that they vouch for you and normally support your business on social media and financially. Need advice or a contact? Ask your brand follower. These followers are can be your real friends, family and tribe of business associates. Their loyalty may be unmatched, but it is always earned.

So how do you create brand followers? Direct contact, building a niche audience, and rewarding that audience will create your group of brand followers. Direct contact, as discussed, involves direct communication in order for your followers to become "friends" or more invested in you and your social content. Direct contact methods include direct messaging, commenting and video or audio messages. If you have a fine group of customers or followers, thank them. They will appreciate your gratitude and know they are buying into the right company, person, and/or brand.

Building a niche audience is a method that involves first knowing your brand and who it serves, then knowing your audience and catering to that audience. But now we're talking about true loyal followers. You create them by giving special offers to these loyal followers and subscribers. This goes above and beyond social media engagement to a higher level of a type of business partnership with you and your followers via providing incentives for customer or follower loyalty. Incentives will keep your fans coming back as they will feel that they matter to you due to your follower incentives like discounts and exclusive access to a product for following or engaging with your brand (Gillian, 2019).

While building your brand, you will soon be able to identify who your leading brand followers are and what they respond to. You may find yourself trying different social media outreach strategies before you gain true brand follower loyalty, however it will be worth it in the end because these fans will stay with your brand and help it to grow through continuously supporting you on social media and buying your products. Engage with your followers and they will become loyal to your brand, offer them something exclusive and they will be brand followers.

33.

Sunshine's Golden Rule: Be Good at Being Your Best Self

It's important to keep in mind that social media strategy is a journey of trial and error. Your strategy should NOT be about emulating another brand's style and content verbatim, nor is it about constantly posting anything that comes to mind. The power to be successful on social media for any brand comes from one important place your own power to be unique. Thus, the secret to social media success lies within you. My golden rule for shining online via social media is to be good at being you. Be great at identifying and presenting your distinctive personal brand.

The same thing applies to your business. Identify and present the brand in the best possible light while staying true to the essence of the brand, which means preserving the individuality and uniqueness of if for those that embrace it, your fans.

Think about what vibe you're giving off and why people are into your brand. Or if people are not into your brand, are you turning people off? When you align your mojo with the essence of your brand, you can then focus on becoming the best version of yourself to present on social media and to your follower base. Remember - you won't be able to please everyone. For example, when transitioning from a personal profile, which attracted friends only, to a personal CEO profile, I discovered that some followers were interested in my CEO brand and others were not. So, if my profile was *not* all about my personal life, some would unfollow, and I would gain new followers for my upgraded brand on social media. Despite losing followers, I began to Shine Online for those followers that enjoyed seeing my brand grow and to new followers interested in media business. (Remember loss of a follower = gain online. You want faithful followers that actually like you, not the opposite.) Shine by being your best you online without fear of not blending in.

Bright Ideas: Ways to Be Your Authentic Self

- Identify your brand and what it stands for beyond gaining profit, these are your values

- Identify your value proposition, this is your unique offering

- Identify your style are you lover of photos or video, choose your way to Shine Online, select a platform and curate your content according to your unique taste and style

- Create a vision and show others how you are creating that path

- If you decide to use photos of influential people or quotes that inspire you on your social media, be sure that your audience understands how their work inspires you for the better.

Chapter 3

Strategies for Using Social Media Tools to Shine Online

Well, is it working? (Your social media app.) Mostly likely it is, if you are using social media on active network.

Every social media tool functions in a different way and has its own distinct features. Understanding what each tool has to offer will help you create valuable content to Shine Online. Effectively employing platform tools optimizes design, flow, and content reach of your site. You will find tips on how to use social media tools throughout this book, but here are specific ways that you can use popular social media tools that are built into the apps to Shine Online and grow your engagement organically.

Take a moment to visit Instagram @LearnMediaToday and www.LearnMediaToday.com for more information on business strategies, live training and coaching or reach out directly at www.sunshinewest.org.

34
Hashtags

Hashtags are pound-sign symbols with a word or phrase following, that are used on social media to create a trending topic and to highlight a subject. Hashtags have become so effective and popular, that they are used for large-scale public relations campaigns. Hashtagged words should be placed *within* or *after* comments to support the subject. Hashtags on social media help you shine by bringing interested and like-minded users to your profile. On Instagram, hashtags are currently limited to 30 per post (2020, Instagram). For Twitter, use specific short-form posts with a focused hashtag or a hashtag on a popular topic. Hashtags also appear on Facebook and other social media platforms; however, they are more useful on platforms like Instagram and Twitter because of how they are commonly used to find topics on these platforms. Hashtags are searchable on Instagram, so it makes them easy to access. Users can scroll through every public #AtlantaPeople post on Instagram and find people interested or experiencing the same thing. Now, users can even follow a hashtag topic on Instagram. Thus, hashtags are becoming a way for social media users to focus on one idea, now consistently and with ease. Use hashtags to help you find people in your community and spark conversations and share ideas and interests. Your engagement can increase with every post when you use hashtags to Shine Online.

My Community Hashtags: #ShineOnline #SunshineInspo #LearnMediaToday #IShineLike

35
Tagging

Tagging helps you connect. Connect to your other business pages or major websites that complement your business.

Tagging is a simple way of shining online via transferring "their followers" to "your followers." The act of tagging itself on social media happens when you utilize a connection tool embedded in social media to connect another user or "tag" them to your profile, story or picture. This tagging allows you to also appear on their social media profile. In the early Facebook days, this was simply a great tool for friends sharing photos of college events and happenings, however tagging is fast becoming a tool for business and growth on social media.

How tagging can work for brands? Imagine having an entire audience of people sharing your product on their profile and tagging you, you are then exposed to more online users who will create a buzz or interest around your brand. Another new way people are using tagging is through stories that appear on Instagram. On Instagram stories, users can tag business brands and other people, making it easy to access a business or brand page with one click while viewing a story.

Tagging can be used to show that you attended an event, have famous friends, or to connect yourself to just about anything. Sometimes it is a great way for people to know who you are connected to. Be cautious and sure that profiles you are tagging to your profile are profiles that you want to be connected with. Also, if the people are tagging you are not in line with your standards, remove the tag or kindly ask to not be tagged in the future. This will prevent off-brand or off the wall tagging situations. The goal is to Shine Online by building a following while sustaining your brand. No intrusions via tagging should be accepted. Facebook now has a privacy setting in which tagged photos must be approved prior to being posted to your Facebook Timeline. The proof is in the pudding. Tagging has power because people will know who you know and possibly, how you know them. This is great for business promotion but can be bad for business when your friend is tagging "Throwback Thursday" posts of your 2006 drunken birthday night out. #BadForBusiness

Tagging, at its best, is used for connection campaigns between other businesses or influencers. This occurs when all members of the campaign understand that they will be tagging in support of an event or social media marketing campaign. The outcome is more shine and followers for all.

RULES TO TAGGING:

Only tag yourself to individuals or brands that you definitely want to be affiliated with.

Do not tag people that prefer not to be tagged or in a way that seems intrusive of their privacy.

Remove or block users that associate you with unwanted tagged photos or posts. If it is not on-brand with your profile, remove it! Don't turn people off with unintended potentially harmful tag associations.

Tags to businesses or brands may need approval, so think before you tag!

Creative ways to use tagging:
- Tag Locations
- Tag Friends, Family, Associates
- Tag prominent people you know
- Tag users to special announcements or sales

36

Sharing on Social Media

Sharing content online occurs anytime you re-post information or broadly share original content. Sharing your own or others' posts creates community and connection. These connections can lead you to shine on through increased exposure. Sharing is essential to social media success because it connects your content with other users and also allows other users the chance to show your content via sharing on platforms. You should associate with brands that will help your brand and "find complementary brands that share your target audience." (Quicksprout.com, 2019).

One example of sharing on Instagram occurs when you post an original story (a special live feed) on Instagram. Your post from your Instagram page or feed can be reposted or shared to your Instagram stories with one click of an arrow button, thereby being exposed to stories viewers another audience. Also, if you are the creator of original content that a user has shared, you will be notified that they shared your content. Thus, sharing has become an increasingly popular move on social media to easily connect users, events and ideas.

Why create something original when you can re-post a quote or an associate's photos of you from their page? All shared posts do not have to be original. In fact, it is popular on Instagram to share others posts in your Instagram stories feed in order to show your support for their posts. For me, sharing others' posts has allowed for greater business connections online because users appreciate me sharing their content.

Overall, sharing is great for business as well as personal use. To shine through sharing on social media, repost positive on-brand content of others as well as your own original content. If you have a public profile, make sure the sharing option is available if you are comfortable with your information being shared with others online.

37

Commenting

Commenting is a form of engagement that is important to growing online because it allows users to easily start a conversation online. These simple conversations could lead to financial conversions later. Commenting itself is one of the easiest ways for you to engage with other users online and listen to your audience. It's an icebreaker that welcomes conversation by saying, "Hi, I am here, and this is what I do." Or you might say, "I like this or that about you." Your target user will want to do two things: 1.) Look at your page to find out about you and, 2.) Reply to you or follow you based on your content or comment. Yes, connecting and engaging to Shine Online can be as simple as commenting to easily gain a new follower or "like" online. Commenting not only connects you with other users, but also exposes your brand to other users who are also reviewing their page.

Whether or not you receive a comment is not always an indication if your brand or post is effective or not. If you haven't asked your audience much or captioned your photo, don't always expect a comment. However, if you are clear on your ideas, have a great photo or ask for some action in your post or caption, you are likely to get a comment or response to your post.

Bright Ideas: Good commenting manners

- When someone comments, as the host of your social media site, it is your job to evaluate their comment as appropriate or not and decide if it stays up on your public posts.

- Secondly, your social media brand will add value and loyalty when you reply to commenter

- When commenting on other's profiles, look for brands that are complementary to your brand, aka others that can help you or that might want what you are offering. Comment in positive ways by giving compliments or stating that you'd like to connect.

- Keep all comments respectful and DO NOT engage in comment fights or bickering with random users online. This can destroy your brand, especially if your words are posted or broadcast in some other way to a larger audience.

38
Social Media Ads & Targeting Your Audience

Targeted advertising, is it cheating? By no means is targeted advertising cheating when it comes to gaining growth online.

Advertising on social media platforms is becoming more user-friendly as well as accessible. Advertising on platforms like Instagram and Facebook provides all the necessary information for each business user or social media manager to create an ad. This information includes free analytics and the ability to pay a little or a lot of money to create ads. Ads don't cost a lot of money, but they do help a lot by targeting your audience.

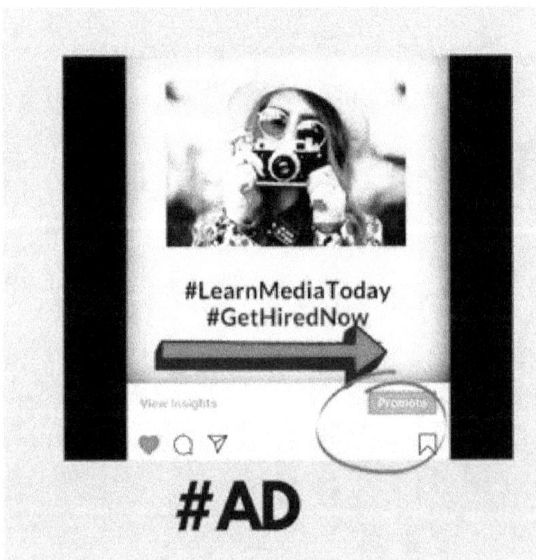

Ads again, should be targeted, because, "you can save a lot of money and time by being intentional in your audience targeting" (Mulvey, 2018). Creating target ad includes thinking of your core demographic audience for your selected post that you will advertise. The targeted ads then will help you to Shine Online as you will appear to your selected audience and gain views on your post/ad. Targeted ads also help you monetize your business or service because the ads become a direct link to your business or service. Ensure your targeted ads have access to pertinent information necessary for a target viewer to know how they can find your service.

For success with ads, you must understand your target demographic and be specific. For example, single moms in Texas with teens who like to eat chicken. I think there is an audience or service for that! Ads help you reach out to that specific or broad audience that is seeking you. You should always evaluate how your targeted as do overtime to see what requires changes, "the trick to audience targeting is to improve your insights into what works overtime" (Mulvey, 2018).

Bright Ideas: Tips for Targeting
- Understand and know your core demographic information
- Demographics might include: Age, gender, location, ethnicity, or special interests
- The more focused your special interests, the more likely your ad is to reach your targeted audience

39
Choose a Type of Profile (Business vs. Private)

Profiles matter and whether you have a business or personal profile could change the way you shine on social media. With private profiles, you are building from within. You are closing yourself off from potential new people that could be interested in your posts. That person with a private profile may not be interested in shining too much, their light is a bit dim to outside users. However, if you are forward-thinking and looking to expand your personal or professional brand, a public profile is best because it enables new users to connect with your brand easily through viewing your posts and connecting with you. If you want to really ramp it up, get a business profile. Even if *you* are your business (i.e. blogger, actor, model), you can still benefit from using a business profile because you will have the ability to create ads and review page analytics daily. A business public profile helps you shine by maximizing your exposure and providing additional tools to connect with your audience. Those tools are discussed more in this list (see #38 Targeted Ads).

40
Instagram Scanners

Now, connecting online is as easy a quick scan. On Instagram, you can create a special scanning tag that allows users to quickly identify and follow you. These scanning tags can be used on websites outside of Instagram in order to promote your brand and gain followers. For example, if you have a business Facebook page, now you can add a photo of your Instagram tag and acquire followers there too. This is a quick and easy way to Shine Online by gaining traction through this easy following method. Instagram scanners are considered S.E.I. (See glossary). As new technology emerges on Instagram and other social media sites, testing useful adds like Instagram scanners as they come out will help you to Shine Online by increasing your exposure and showing that you are keeping up with up-and-coming changes online.

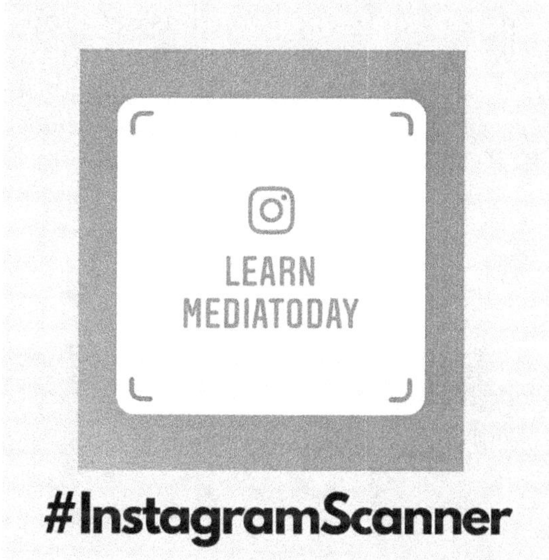

41
Search Engine Optimization (SEO)

SEO on website and social media like blogs, direct people to you and what you do while they are searching the world wide web. One of the most valuable things that a company can do is to have SEO in place on their websites because it draws customers to them and their brands. SEO uses keyword text to allow audiences to identify you online and affects your ranking on important search engines like Google. SEO is crucial for blogs and websites that are linked to other social media. A ranking website is the first to be seen, the first to be viewed, clicked and sold to customers. Be first by using SEO to make your brand shine to the top of search engines, letting your customers know who you are without having to do too much digging.

In order to implement SEO, I used my website builder's SEO section and added key words about my business so that if people search for those words my name and business will appear in the search engine. If you are not familiar with how implement SEO using key words, find an SEO expert or logon to www.learnmediatoday. com for webinar to get your started implementing SEO for your brand's blog or website. (See also the last section on monetization.)

#SEO

42
Connect Your Brand Across Platforms

Connecting your brand across platforms occurs when your social media pages are synced, linked and on-brand. Connect your Instagram posts to Facebook, Tumblr and Twitter pages. One great aspect of cross-platform connections is that you do not have to post the same thing three or four times on all of your social media networks. Cross-platform connecting makes it easy to maintain your own social media networks and post consistently on your pages.

One important aspect to remember is that each network works differently, but that doesn't necessarily mean that you lose brand quality as you post across different platforms. Keep your brand consistent but adjust to the styles of different platforms. For example, on Instagram, you can post both microblogs and long- form posts with a tremendous amount of information captioned under each post. On the flip side, Twitter has a 280-character limit, currently up from the previous 140-character limit, so the expectation is short and sweet posts that get to the point and are sharable. In fact, some of the most clever and popular posts are ones where the poster minimized their writing and made their point in a direct and humorous way. So, change your style to meet the platform, but keep your brand message the same. If you find yourself caught up in Twitter comment wars, veering off-brand or posting with no purpose, pause, and return to branding and shining online the right way.

If you would like some examples, review a popular brand's social media across various platforms. Discover how they are using each platform to maximum potential while staying on-brand. Cross-platform connection is a valuable tool and a requirement in today's social media marketing world. Don't get caught in the trap of over-posting on all platforms, as you might discover that you shine best to your audience on certain ones, and that's great! But do not hesitate to take the journey across to other platforms as you might find additional Shine Online with users that you might have never reached, had you not shared your brand on other social media sites.

Chapter 4

Strategies for Creating Media to Shine Online

"How do I look?" You will likely be asking yourself this after you post your first YouTube video. But before posting or even creating, there are things you should know. Quality gets you views. This section is created to provide strategies on creating high-quality visual media content for social media pages that will help you to Shine Online.

Remember, your media doesn't have to be perfectly produced the first time, but it should progressively improve as you get used to the process of creating content. My experiences on camera as a film actress, journalist, as well as behind the scenes as a media producer informs the media strategies below. You can apply these digital media production strategies too, at home, to Shine Online and build your following.

43
Create Quality Photos for Your Brand:
Aesthetics Matter

The rise of popular photo-based social media platforms like Instagram are proof-positive that users love visuals more than anything else. The key to any social media star's success will inevitably include a photo, whether it's a photo of themselves,　a product or service in action. The quality photo is the basis for building a brand. Just think about it, before a user dips into the content of your timeline, they'll look first check out your profile photo. Lightly scrolling through the first three to six pictures on Instagram might determine if they keep looking. If I am not a supermodel or genius photographer, how do I shine on social media using photos?

Many of the creative ways you can use photos will be discussed later in the list.

To start, here are tips to create captivating photos online:

#QualityPhoto

Creating a photo that is quality in nature involves a bit of technical know-how. Even if you have the best story to tell in your photo caption, if you photo is not quality or off putting in some way you are not Shining Online. However, when you present a quality well- lit, interesting photo, you attract new audiences to your profile. You do not have to be a professional photographer to achieve this. You only have to apply yourself using modern tools to display your life or brand via photos. Note the branding techniques in this section and book for quality in your photo content but here are some ways to have a technically sound quality photo:

1. Use daylight for your photos. This is most inexpensive but effective light source.

2. Avoid being "back lit" or having your body in front of a light source. Make sure the light is on your face or the subject of the photo rather than behind it.

3. Try a bright light like a ring light for indoor selfies and special photos.

4. Ask for help. Try asking a friend to take your photo rather than only posting selfies. Also, a professional photographer can be used for special branded photos.

#BrandedPhoto

Make sure your brand is reflected in every photo if possible. There's nothing wrong about being spontaneous like celebrating milestones, but no matter how tempting, let's not post a negative meme of your ex on your feed. You're probably going off-brand! To stay on-brand, ask yourself what you want to represent? Women in business, bikers from Florida, New York lawyers, or chefs from California? Whatever it is, make your pictures reflect that and you will begin to shine in your area of focus.

#StoryPic

Let a photo tell your story. Just picture: A celebrity football player in South America jumps from a nature cliff into a beautiful blue pond with exotic surroundings. This outstanding picture is worth a thousand words. Of course, not every picture will have this sort of setting, but some photos should tell a story of something special that happened and how it supports your personal or professional brand.

#TheLook

Design your look by having consistent filters or a few go-to filters and backgrounds in your photos help to get your brand idea across. For example, an earthy traveler might use the well-known "Hefe" filter on Instagram to express his rugged lifestyle climbing mountains and walking our country's nature trails. A fashion designer might prefer a clean crisp filter, with high contrast visual effects, that expresses their love for clean lines and high fashion.

Photos have taken the social media world to the next level of visual representation. Now more than ever, you have the power to shine on social media using photos as a means of expression, storytelling and brand imagery. With your brand and goals in mind, post quality and on-brand photos to peak interest with new audiences, engage your followers and Shine Online.

44
Online Pre-Recorded Videos: Get Subscribers

Producing online videos has become extremely valuable to the content creators as well as their audiences. Audiences have easy access to information and subscriptions, while the creator has a simple but useful way of connecting their ideas. Shine Online by using video content to speak directly to your audience about you, your brand, or area of expertise.

Video platforms like YouTube make it fairly easy to start creating a brand name and post videos online. To start, you should think of what you have to say, who it will help and why they will listen. This is the path to making effective videos to build a brand with influence. It's your job to figure out the "why," the reason to watch and your target audience.

Platforms that are helpful for creating your video empire include YouTube, Instagram TV, Facebook Watch, Vimeo, SnapChat, and any blogs sites where videos can be posted. However, if you are focused on gaining subscribers and a fans for your videos, then you will need to going with YouTube is your best option. With YouTube, fans can subscribe to your network online and be led to your unique services using links attached to your videos.

The great thing about pre-recorded videos versus live videos is that you can edit them to make them better. Now many phones have editing programs build into them like iMovie, but if your mobile device does not have an editing program there are tons of apps online for editing including those discussed in strategy #46. Remember to include text and graphics to support your ideas as well and make your video shining, entertaining and memorable for your audience.

Bright Idea: The key to Shining Online using video is to infuse your brand and valuable content into your videos. With each video, have a goal in mind such as gaining increased subscriptions or leading your audience to watch another video or make a purchase by visiting your website.

45
Live Videos: Go Live, Speak Up.

"Lives" or live videos will grow your social media exponentially because they expose your audience to you in a very personal but public way. Your audience will be taken with your real personality, your soft spots and your strengths, and they will *want* to engage with you and truly become your fan. It is also becoming more common for communities of like-minded individuals to gather online. For example, if you have an organic hair product and your followers are also interested in it, the live feed can serve as a discussion forum or meeting to discuss their common interest. Lives pull in more viewers by increasing your appearance in special places on social media timelines and notifying your followers that you have posted a live video.

Use of live video is an excellent channel through which you can collaborate with other brands. For example, brands host forums on social media featuring multiple brands on live feeds as "live events." Live social media events occur when a live social media video session is pre-planned and advertised (normally on social media) and carried out by one or more brands. These live video collaborations are highly beneficial because of the exposure to double or triple the number of followers.

Instagram, Facebook, and YouTube are platforms that are known for their live feeds because they highlight live videos to your followers and enable you to access your video in real-time or later once you've stopped going live.

Bright Ideas: A Few Tips for Live Video

- Ensure your audience can hear and see you clearly.
- Don't forget about your background, your clothing and overall setting. Remember, it's live!
- Add value and be engaging. (If you want people to come back again.)
- If it is a special event, mention when you will be going live. So your followers can know when to tune-in on their social media live feeds.

46
Apps, Use Helpful Apps for Social Media Content:

Apps can be extremely helpful to you in developing content and ideas to make your social media shine. An app like Boomerang offers tools like special effects video. In addition, there are apps that offer photo editing, photo layouts, digital effects, graphics and various photo or video manipulations. Use these apps to enhance the meaning of your content and bring it to life. Apps with filters and other digital effects can also be helpful when you are trying to create a curated look that will help you Shine Online.

Quite often, folks fall into the trap of overusing photo editing apps, which can do a disservice to their brand. For example, I try not to overuse the Layout app (which displays small portions of photos) for posted photo collection. I prefer my branded photos to appear full size on social media. However, I find the Layouts and similar apps useful for posts about special events where there are many photos and lots of people. Ensure the app that you use enhances visibility and your branding efforts to gain influence, followers and Shine Online.

Recommended Media Content Apps:
1. FaceTune – photo editing
2. Boomerang – special effects video
3. Layout – photo collage app
4. iMovie -video editing
5. VivaVideo- video and special effects
6. Magisto- quick video editing with effects
7. BIGVU- teleprompter/video recording
8. Canva- graphics
9. Ripl – 1-minute video & motion graphics

47
Original Graphics (User Created)

Creative News Flash! You do not have to be a trained graphic artist to showcase quality graphics on your social media page. Canva and other graphics programs make it easy to create colorful visuals for your brand. Use a graphic template app to create the desired quality and look for your brand. Once you decide on your brand, use graphic apps to create complementary ads. The more attractive your graphics content, the more you will shine on social media. Refer to strategy #46 for recommended apps and #13 for branding strategies which should all go into your original graphics. For more information on how you can become your own Ad and post maker on social media sign-up for my course Ad Design on a Dime. If decide to create your own graphic content not only will your brand shine with originality, but you will also save some cash, which you could use for other things in your branding budget.

48
Professional Graphics & Logo:

If you want professional visuals or a designed logo, find a professional graphic artist to assist you in bringing your branding ideas to life. A logo should reflect you or your brand with a few or no words. Using symbols and colors, create a logo that appeals to broad audiences in way a that makes you or your brand instantly identifiable. Even if you employ a professional, incorporate the "power of you" and *your* creativity when finalizing logos and graphics and to ensure they are on-brand and consistent with your message. For videos and tools about where to find professionals and the process of creating logos and branding material head to Instagram @LearnMediaToday today and visit our websites for free training.

49
Use Video Production Techniques: Lights, Camera, Action!

Social media videos are one of the single most powerful ways to Shine Online. Social media video formats include live, short-form and recorded videos. (Live and short-form videos are addressed in strategies #45 and #50.) Pre-recorded video can seriously impact your brand (#44).

I remember one of my first times posting a video on social media for my media production company 20-West Entertainment & Media LLC., I quickly discovered how my audience liked my content by views, likes and comments. Over time, I discovered new audiences, previously unaware of me. This is the power of video. No matter if your video is instructional, inspirational, or pure entertainment, it works. However, the most effective video should be a quality product that conveys your message with little effort from the viewer.

Free video, the holy grail of the Internet, does what all entrepreneurs and influencers should do – add value without asking for anything in return.

Thus, even if you are preaching the best gospel on the planet in your videos, it won't matter if the audience can't see you or hear you. Invest in tools to create a quality video. That would include a good mobile phone camera or quality digital camera with good audio output. Test your camera and lighting **prior** to making your full video to avoid re-recording it. If natural lighting is not sufficient, use lighting kits or a ring light to make yourself visible on camera.

Here are a few tools that you need for quality video production online:
- Quality content, that adds value
- Quality lighting
- Microphone for audio quality if not sufficient from your phone/camera
- Reasonable setting (Backdrop, plan wall, nature)
- Editing program for your videos (i.e. Final Cut Pro, iMovie)

Learning to make a quality video involves trial and error. Even the most experienced journalists and actors fumble on camera and forget their lines. Media producers also learn and improve their quality gradually with each shoot. Take the steps to create a quality video to Shine Online using the proper tools and learning good techniques for speaking and production.

For additional training on video production, photography and lighting, head to Instagram @LearnMediaToday today and visit our websites for training.

50
Micro Video

Short-form video is a quick way to help you Shine Online. Videos under two minutes are advantageous because you will get your message across without boring the viewer or wasting any of their precious time. Take the food prep, "Tasty" brand videos. Tasty videos are short-form videos with some as short as 30 seconds. These videos took over social media in 2017, proving that something as complex as cooking could be simplified on video. This simplification made the Tasty videos hugely popular on social media. Another short-form video is the micro-video like those found on the app Vine. Vine-style micro- videos are super-efficient in conveying messages and entertaining ideas. Being short and sweet guarantees that your audience will actually watch it because the video is over before they get distracted. Short-form videos will garner views while quickly sharing your message and having the impact you want. Short-form videos are great for entertainment, stories, and promotions. Try them to get a quick shine and tally up your view counts.

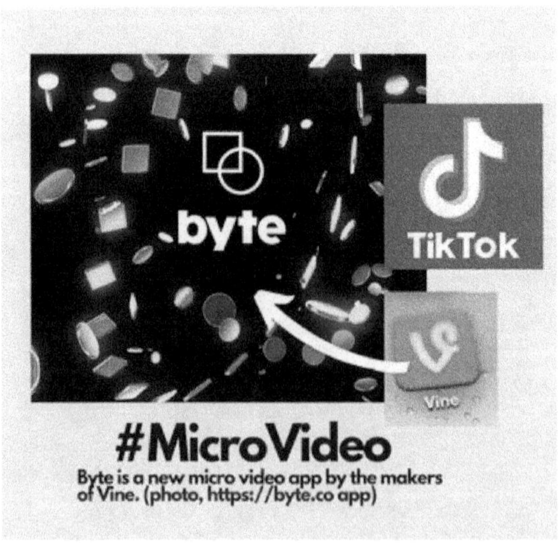

Byte is a new micro video app by the makers of Vine. (photo, https://byte.co app)

51
Teleprompters: Shine on Camera

If you dread getting in front of the camera to verbalize your message and/or you're not good at ad-libbing, teleprompters and apps like BigVu are at your rescue. Teleprompter apps, like BigVu, used in conjunction with your smartphone or digital notebook allow you to load pre-typed text into the app, so you then can read aloud in your videos. Before you know it, you'll go from being an amateur to a shining YouTuber.

In my experience using an iPad teleprompter was the best and easiest way to make a video online with a lot of points. I've also used real teleprompters in a broadcast news studio as a news intern/journalist at a major television network in Atlanta. Although the studio cameras are much larger, the ones that you will use at home with an iPad will function in similar way, by scrolling text on screen at a selected pace. The trick is to know your content pretty well and keep going, even if you stumble, remember you can edit the video later. (See also strategy #46 for apps with teleprompter and editing capabilities.)

#Teleprompters

Bright Ideas: How to Look good on Camera

- Express yourself- Even if you are not a pageant girl, like me, try smiling or expressing yourself in the video.

- "Cheat" to the Camera- When interviewing someone never completely turn your face away from the camera for a long duration in a two or more person on-camera interview.

- Wear Color- Wear a simple color that stands out but won't be distracting. Anything you wear can work but be sure it doesn't distract too much from what you are saying.

- Speak Slowly- This is not to speak in an unnatural way, but if you are not a great speaker or stumble a lot this will help your speech sound a bit clearer.

52
Specialized Effects & Photo Strategy

One way to make your photos and videos Shine Online is to present them from a fresh, new perspective. For example, instead of your typical selfie, have a friend take a side shot of your face and show the background of where you are, then use a special filter to make it stand out. This is a creative strategy to catch the eye. Also, consider posting black and white, uniquely lit or partially blurred photos that will help you stand out, shine and continue to build interest with your followers online. Many apps offer special effects and custom filters to enhance your media and message in order for you to Shine Online. Special effects in your photos including motion graphics, help you to build interest because they catch the eye. Shine Online using fun effects and graphics on your story feeds and timelines. (See strategy #46 for apps with graphic capability).

53

Music: Turn it Up, Use Music to Stand Out

Music associated with content is a great tool to awaken your online audience. Music itself adds interest and connects communities. If your community prefers a certain genre of music, it is to your advantage to play that type of music to accompany content. For example, to hype up your Instagram stories you can now add your favorite song to a simple video post. More commonly, music is used for creative photo montages, video promotions and talent showcases. Don't worry about music interrupting someone's office day because most social media sites, including Instagram, have quick audio controls. However, typical online users (with headphones) will enjoy your multi-media post and experience your message both visually and auditorily.

54
Live Stories & Live Streaming Networks

Social media is a fluid, rapidly evolving medium, so being proactive about new social media structures and software programs is an important strategy. Embrace and implement these changes to keep up with the rest of the world and move your social media following to the next level.

One example of an emerging change in social media includes social media platforms now acting as full streaming networks. Facebook's new video streaming extension, Facebook Watch was a huge success for actress Jada Pinkett-Smith's show Red Table Talk, because of Facebook's instant audience of millions of users combined with Pinkett-Smith's influence. Now, anyone with a Facebook page and lengthy video content can add their video to the Facebook Watch streaming network.

#InstagramStories

Live stories as discussed in this book are popular on the social media platforms Facebook and Instagram, with about 500 million users interacting with Instagram stories daily (Scott, 2019). Leverage stories to Shine Online by using them to supplement or add interest to your Instagram feed. When you post a story feed, use it to announce important content you will present on your pages or to inform your audience of important happenings. If you have over 10,000 followers, you can even link your Instagram stories feed to a page to outside websites that lead to your business page or blog page, using the "swipe up" feature. Shine using the emerging technology of live stories and live streaming.

As new digital media technologies and features develop on social media you must decide which ones you need to adapt in order to sustain or improve your brand. Being on every network, all the time is not required. Yet, doing exceptionally well on one or two networks is a must for your brand. Decide on your network, mediums and media content strategies to create your brand. Adapt to changes as they develop to continue to Shine Online.

For additional training on digital media production and social media content creation strategies or training head to Instagram @ LearnMediaToday today and visit our websites for training www.SunshineWest.org and www.LearnMediaToday.com.

Chapter 5

The Strategic List for Creating Shining Content

What makes great, perfect and beautiful content on social media? That depends on the eye of the beholder, in our case, the follower. For example, some users are into funny cat memes, while others are following their favorite pop star like Beyoncé, never missing a single post. So, you don't like cats and you are not a pop star. How can your content stand out? The secret to great content is to create based on what you represent and what others will appreciate. Will they follow you? Yes, if they like it, you are a shining star to them.

Shining & Creative Content

55
Funny Memes & Photo Text Combos

When it comes to content, memes are creative ways to entertain your audience or get your point across. Memes consist of a photo or cartoon coupled with a witty text meant to entertain the viewer of the post. Although memes are known as mindless entertainment in the Internet of comedy, memes can serve a purpose. Sometimes memes are used to make an interesting point using comedy. Other times they are used only to entertain. Whatever your goals, memes are great content ideas and can include any photo/text combination that conveys an intended message.

To shine using memes think about your brand. If your social media page focuses on politics commentary or other social issues, an occasional meme can provide entertainment relief about otherwise serious issues. Memes can also highlight the ironic nature of an issue. Choose carefully and ensure your meme is not offensive. If your meme is meant to be controversial, be sure you know the controversy it can bring and be prepared to hear about it from your online audience.

Entertaining Commentary
Attracts an Audience.

On the bright side, photo text combo posts do not have to be considered a meme. Photo/text combo posts are any posts with   a combination of photo and text meant to convey an idea. These types of posts can have just about any topic to promote your brand. I use photo text posts to encourage and inspire my audience in the areas of media marketing and entrepreneurship. These posts are very helpful when building a brand because the instantly add value. The viewer does not even have to scroll to your comments section to see what you are hoping to say, they know what you represent by your branded post using photo with you message. Shine Online using entertaining and promotional photo/text posts, your audience will instantly connect and be entertained by you.

#Meme

56
Show Off Your Talents

Ask yourself: What can you do? Can it be displayed online? If so, how?

Showcasing your unique talent as a gifted musician, artist, painter, dancer, or chef online via video, blog or another type of post is a great way to gain a tribe of people that are fans of your talent or want to learn from you. It's no fun to review a singer's profile, for example, and never actually see them sing or perform. If you have talent, put it out there because if you don't you may come across as being unauthentic. Yes, it's a bold move, but a worthy one. When you showcase your talent, you will build fans overnight. It is your choice how, when and where to present it on social media, but once you do, you'll shine and grow in your confidence showing off your talents.

#Art

Art by the Author, Sunshine West.

57
Breaking News Content

Post consistently about news or content that matters to users in your field of business.

Posting news on social media is a valuable way to find success online. Why? People that follow you may begin to depend on you as a source for news and information. Entertainment news is also great content to present, which will keep your audience coming back for more. Where there is news, there are viewers wanting to be informed. News provides a great bit of shining content to present online, either as primary or intermittent posts because your audience will continuously consume it and appreciate your presentation of information.

58
Politics for Engagement

Posts about politics are specific and will draw followers and viewers to your profile, creating easy Shine Online. Unfortunately, this crowd can be angrily opposing or highly supportive. This is because posting about politics is emotionally charged. The topic of politics is a combination of valuable, controversial and irresistible content, making political content highly sought after. Whether you are posting about your political opinions or hard facts, your content *will* be questioned by an opposing force. If you choose to post about politics, consistently, you must develop a thick skin and consider controversy the engagement you need to keep your page going. In fact, most effective political posts will elicit a response from supporters and possibly those that may not support your political point of view. If you are simply posting facts or something neutral, don't be surprised if followers engage in their own conversations using your post as a digital meeting place for a debate. The great news is that you have the power as the poster of the social media, to moderate responses and create a safe space for your followers and supporters. Remember, sowing discord intentionally online can land you in trouble, however, sharing political news and starting conversations may create desired engagement that your page needs.

59
History & Historical Significance

History-related posts, especially on celebrated or significant dates, illuminate your social media by showing authenticity through sharing historical dates that you know and care about with your followers. History is the preface to the present, so any historical significance that is on-brand and of interest to your audience is worthy of posting. However, when it comes to history there are a few important things to remember: 1.) Be factual and research the facts. 2.) Be respectful by not adding a loaded story to known history. 3.) Be timely, especially for historical events where the date is important. However, if the post is not date-specific history, post away. If posting about history be sure to speak up about history that matters and that is significant to your brand and inform gracefully with full respect to content, relevance and accuracy.

60
Empowerment and Inspirational Content II

Empowerment and inspirational posts are among the most sought-after and supported posts on social media, with the hashtag, #inspiration, showing 150 million posts on Instagram and #empowerment showing 5.9 million posts as of September 2019. So, why inspire your audience? Inspiration and personal empowerment are a top social media strategy because it is a form of adding value. Adding value is when the audience gains something helpful from engaging with or viewing your social media posts.

Inspirational posts, can be much like going to church, listening to a guest speaker, or attending a seminar, because it acts as a value token to the viewer of the post. For every niche audience and online user, there is a point of attraction through inspiration. The key is to find or create the inspirational posts that appeals to your audience. This could include posts empowering women, business owners or vegans. It is totally up to you and your brand, but inspiration sells and attracts likes. Likes support your brand, and if you inspire enough people, they will believe in your brand.

Tips for Posting Inspiration:

- **Stay on Brand-** Stay on-brand with your inspiration style, including content and graphic style of quoted graphic posts.

- **Give Credit- It** is easy to find and legally duplicate inspirational posts online; however, if there is a famous quote and you know the author, use it in the post to give credit where it is due ("Reposting" or sharing a post on Instagram is an easy way to provide credit to an original poster of content.)

- **Don't Offend-** Unless you are into tough love, it is not necessary to consistently offend through somewhat inspirational posts. Keep the audience in mind while being authentic to your brand. Remember as my mom might say "You will get more with honey than with lemons."

ï **Promote-** Encourage sharing and liking the post as a call to action to enhance the reach of your post.

An empowering photo or infographic post will instantly attract people looking for inspiration and allow you to Shine Online. Be sure to use hashtags to draw in those that are interested in being inspired. #InspiredProfessional #BusinessBabes #Creatives

61
Add Mystery Posts & Teasers

Have a product coming out? Try posting teasers or interesting posts letting your audience know that something is coming up without giving it all away. Teaser posts or any post that piques mystery or intrigue are sure to help you Shine Online because the audience will continue to peep back and forth to see what's coming next. Using great graphics or posting a set of three or more "grouped posts" on Instagram that create one idea also creates a mysterious but engaging effect to your audience. One important thing about teaser posts is to follow up with your audience. Next, watch their appreciation for you as they follow your journey online and entertain their appetite for mystery.

62
Post Industry Content

Are you a specialist at something, perhaps a data analyst, real estate agent or meal prep/nutritionist? Whatever your industry, if you want to build a niche audience, try industry-specific posts. Industry- specific posts are social media posts that pertain to your career field or business sector and are of value to others in your industry. It might also be helpful to think of industries that complement your industry so that you can connect with those that you would like to work with as well. Shine by posting less-seen industry content. Remember, hashtags are the great connector of industries.

63
Heart Centered Family & Parent Blogs

Are you a mom with an out-of-this-world routine that you'd like to share with your followers and potential customers via social media? The rise of mom blogs is ongoing and where there is a mother needing advice or a connection, there is a follower that appreciates your content.

Yet, family and parent social media posts are not limited to mom blogs but are often used to connect your audience to who you are outside of your job or business. A photo with your family or your child shows the audience what you are working for and who you are under the surface. If you have children, well, then you inevitably have an exciting and busy life. You can post about it if it works with your brand.

Don't have kids? No problem. I personally like posting photos with best friends who are like family, my parents, siblings, and my cute little nephew on occasion to show my audience those who matter to me outside of my business. Many of my followers know my mother, because she was always at acting auditions and business ventures with me. In the past, people liked my posts about her more than myself, because she was known as the cool mom! To really shine through close friends and family posts, pay it forward by telling a valuable story or sharing a special memory where your family picture can be worth a thousand words.

#Fam

64
Special Moments & Epic Times

The truth about social media is that most people are using it to actually be social, to find a sense of belonging, and to stay in touch with those that they know. To many, social media means sharing moments that are semi-public and special to them. One way you can leverage the "social" in social media is by sharing special moments like travel and trips, weddings, engagements, births, celebrations, milestone birthdays, award ceremonies, premieres, performances and meeting important people.

Take your posts to the next level to Shine Online by using creative ways of posting these events. One example discussed earlier in the book is the use of live feeds like Instagram or Facebook Stories. During events post using stories in order to engage your audience an make them feel as if they are there with you (Scott, 2019). Or after the event use your high-quality photos to impress your audience and share your wonderful life experience or accomplishment. Remember, the look and how you present the event is important. Be authentic, but always remember your brand.

65
Take a Selfie (Close-up, Attractive Photos)

Posting a uniquely attractive photo is a popular content point on Instagram. First, posting attractive photos does not mean that you need to be a supermodel. Attractive photos are any photos that present you in a positive light. Got an interview? Post a photo in your suit, letting your followers see you in your shining moment. These attractive photos should have a few elements that will help you to Shine Online: 1.) Use quality visuals helps you to be seen clearly. 2.) Feature your subject or subjects front and center. 3.) Add creativity by using a filter or special theme to add interest and create a bit more shine than an average photo. Your shining posts depend on what you put into them. Be sure to reflect confidence and creativity in your posts all about yourself, especially in selfies.

66
Post Special Accomplishments

Posting about a special accomplishment on social media is a clear way to Shine Online. Who wouldn't want to relive a moment where they are honored and celebrated in style? But don't stop at just posting a photo of yourself receiving an award. Tell your audience the story behind it and make sure the photo is candid, showing you at the event and giving the audience a feel for the level of achievement through visual means. Create a captivating caption with your post to hack the Instagram algorithm by having users review your post for a longer time.

67
Travel: Show Your Journey

Travel is a fun content idea. When you travel either for vacation or work, you have a load of new creative content at your fingertips. All you have to do is take in the sights and sounds and remember, while you are having fun and sporting your 'travel best' clothing, to take photos. Travel blogs are among the most popular microblogs on social media like Instagram. This is because a picture again, is worth many words and when we travel, our scenery and happy vibes create magnetic photos that become the envy and interest of all who view them.

Here are a few tips to ramp up your travel photos for social media blogging:

- Go to dream places that are unique to the region.
- Tell people what the location or special monuments means to you.

ï Capture the scenery around you using unique perspective and wide camera shots to capture the essence of how it feels to be where you are.

68
Share Couples & Partnership Posts

There is a statistic out there stating that happy couples get the least likes on social media because people find happy couples boring. Well, I beg to differ. For some, it almost seems like being in a couple is a form of celebrity marked by extra social media likes for doing--- well just about anything together. A blog created by you and your spouse, partner or bestie is great content because people are drawn to togetherness. Your warm friendship and connection allows others to believe in connectivity in society and makes them feel that they are a part of your journey. Whoever your partner is, just make sure you agree on appearing in your social media posts. The best couple and partnership posts are ones where the couples share some experience that might be interesting or add value to others. That's what people want to see, collective gathering with purpose.

69
Share Your Unique Culture

Have you heard of: "Doing it for the culture?" If you are from somewhere with a unique and flamboyant culture, you have a great platform to share because social media loves culture. Think of Rihanna celebrating at Caribbean festivals or locals enjoying Mardi Gras in New Orleans, my hometown. Special culture is well-liked on social media and helps you and your culture shine in a positive light. Displaying flags, cultural cuisine and art forms are all fair game for the posting. Shine Online through sharing your own special culture and presenting it to your online audience with all the color your culture represents. Always remember that sharing cultural posts are a celebration of who you and others in that culture are. Your culture post educates and informs others outside of that culture. Any and all cultural sharing should be done by those belonging to that culture or those that wish to share facts about or celebrate that culture.

70
Celebrate Who You Are

Celebrating special groups like disabled, minority, LGBQT or another diverse group is something that many niche followers and new followers appreciate. You know, not everyone will have your unique perspective on life, so it is important to express yourself, while also educating others. By being in a special group or subset of culture, you are unique and attractive to those that can celebrate with you. One great idea is to take advantage of special holidays and events to use as photo and video content for your social media. Your audience will thank you for highlighting who you are in a positive light and impacting your community in a positive way.

Posts about who you are show authenticity and help you build a connected, like-minded audience.

71

Awareness

Awareness posts on social media include posts that raise awareness of causes that you support.

You can bring light to a health or humanitarian issue that you support. In addition, these posts can highlight a charity and charitable events. Awareness posts put the spotlight on volunteers and your cause in a way that will spark interest in the cause. Thus, awareness posts create shine for your cause, giving your audience a window into an aspect of your brand that they are sure to remember.

72
Business: Create a Business Tribe

Business-related posts are posts that reflect what your business does and how it can help others. Business posts contain anything from a list of your services to a chart showing industry-specific stats that you want to share. The idea with business posts is to keep your audience engaged about the business or industry your social media page represents.

Remember to think creatively and don't repost so much that every post is a repost of another page's business post. Original content allows you to shine because you are adding real value and it shows off your brand's unique graphic style. If you decide to post mostly about business, understand that it is okay to go off-book and post something personal, but if your core audience consists of business followers, remember that and don't get so personal it turns off your followers.

Consistency is also important with business post content. Posting consistently will help you to continue to attract followers in your industry and keep them. Shine with business content which will help you to create a tribe or loyal following around your business.

Bright Ideas: Business Post Design Tip

Often businesses create photos that include graphics and text combos like mini infographics. This style attracts the eye, while also conveying other important information about your business. Make sure the information is easy to see and understand for quick reading online.

73
Share Spiritual Knowledge & Content

In today's "awakened" society, spiritual knowledge (a subset of inspirational content) is very popular and sought after. Spiritual content posts can include a graphic quote post, video or micro blog that expands on spiritual knowledge. These types of posts reap a faithful following of supporters looking to learn and be inspired. If this is not your main thing, an occasional authentic inspirational/ spiritual post will boost viewership due to the popularity of the genre.

If you are a spiritualist and on social media, shine via offering free spiritual advice on your social media. If your advice is positive and appealing, it will help you retain clients.

#Zen

74
Showcase Special Skills

What is the difference between the skills showcase vs. the talent showcase content strategy? Well, some people have a learned skill that isn't a talent that they were born with. For example, someone with a singing voice can post themselves singing, displaying both talent and skill, versus a music teacher who can share how he developed the skill of playing the piano without necessarily focusing on his talent. According to dictionary.com, a skill is: A craft, trade, or job requiring manual dexterity or special training in which a person has competence and experience. *The importance of talent vs. skill is how you display it.* While a talent might be displayed in a raw or theatrical sense, a skill might be more complex to present or include a mode of instruction if your aim is to train your audience

Shine Online by showcasing your skills by either telling your audience how to learn that skill or displaying it as content. For example, one could display their cooking skills by showing their audience how to properly cut veggies and noting the position your hand should be in while in the act of chopping. Today, users are reviewing social media like YouTube for instruction and there is much space for you to showcase skills. Shine by knowing your skills and sharing them with the world online.

75
Train Your Audience

Training posts are designed to either inform or teach an audience. Training posts shine on social media because they present a form of value to your audience. Think of your audience's point of view when *before* creating training posts. What do they need to know? And what is the best way to say it? Make sure your training content isn't dry and boring. Create your posts to entice the viewer by being graphically sound or attractive to the eye. Training can be a fun and exciting experience depending on the trainer's presentation.

You can also use training posts to tease the audience with valuable information, then ask them to review further information by leading them to review your blog or training event. The key is effective training posts is adding value. That, in turn, creates the demand for what your training has to offer and will push loyalty and faithful following online. Offering free value with training content, again can lead to paying clients when you have an offer for them. Thus, shine by sharing your training content. Review how people respond and shine by understanding the value you add or what you change.

76
Special Day of the Week Posts:
Throwbacks, Flashbacks, etc.

Throwback Thursday, Flashback Friday, Motivation Monday and similar forms are all ways to make a very typical day of the week akin to a holiday. The phenomenon of celebrating a typical day of the week as a special day is certainly the birth child of the Internet and social media. Typically, on a day like Flashback Friday for example, a social media user will post a photo from their past (including recent past) as a form of entertaining or educating their audience. The great thing about these "special day" posts is that they are a great excuse to post anything, especially something about your past like when you got your degree or achieved a life milestone. This is a great way to highlight your credibility and background in specific areas.

Special day of the week posts can feature fun times and highlights in your life or how far you have come. Whatever your highlight, these compelling posts receive traction and likes. So, keep it fun and creative without giving too much away. Your audience will appreciate getting to know you better and delight in your confidence to show off your past and how it helped you to create your present success.

#MotivationMonday

#FriYay rather than #Friday

77
Team Collaboration & Groups

One of the things people find attractive on social media is understanding comradery within a group of team members. Any small business CEO that highlights the group that makes them better is a winner online. Why? Not only will the team feel gratified and appreciated, but others will look at that leader as a supporter and collaborator rather than another ruler in the corporate arena that they'd never have the guts to eat lunch with. Even if you are not a business owner and you highlight a meet-up or other significant group, your collaborative synergy will shine and might even attract new members to you. The key is to be respectful, balanced inclusive as possible when showing off how your group works. Your team then, will want to share the posts and therefore, share more information about you and/or your brand, helping you to Shine Online. As they say, "teamwork makes the dream work." The same applies on social media.

78
Friendships

Are you who you hang out with? The answer is "yes" on social media.

Highlighting professional or personal friendships with individuals acts as an extension of you and your brand. People, including bloggers, are paying attention to whom you follow and who is following you. High-quality friends are crucial because they will support you and show off your brand. If you feel like your friends could be a threat to your brand, you might want to keep them off any business social media account. The upside of posts with friends is sharing great moments and showing off the support system you are connect with. In the age of a digitally isolated society, people love to be part of something bigger than themselves, they seek out the feelings of unity that your friendship posts provide, and that is a powerful builder of trust in you.

79
Share Your Fab Lifestyle

Lifestyle posts consist of social media that allow followers and viewers to see a glimpse into the life (food, style, locations) of the poster. Normally, lifestyle posts are presented in a more stylish way than the average post about life's happenings. The aim of most lifestyle bloggers is to gain a following or sell a product or service.

Lifestyle social media content encompasses a broad spectrum of ideas. Many popular lifestyle posters present strategic styling of food, fashion or home. Lifestyle photos are attained by professional or near-professional photography that result in quality visually appealing posts on a regular basis.

Lifestyle posts are hugely popular and can be integrated with a large amount of business ideas. The key idea is to help your audience understand how viewing your lifestyle posts is valuable to them. Perhaps the audience is inspired by your lifestyle and wants to integrate your home organization techniques or fashionable style into their own lives. Whatever the reason they tune-in, lifestyle posts will boost your social media following, which could mean gains later if you decide to monetize your social media.

Bright Ideas: Tips for Lifestyle Content

1. Use quality photos. (Strategy #43)

2. Create a goal with your posts.

3. Engage with your audience and followers to build loyalty.

80
Repost & Share Content

Reposts are great and easy content to post on social media. Reposts are posts that are shared by you, because they are either include you or the value of the content aligns with your message enough to share it. Reposts provide the opportunity to share while easily crediting the original poster of the content. Typically, individuals repost from people they know or are familiar with in order to give them their photo credit. When reposting, make sure it is content that source of the post would not mind your sharing it. Also, verify the post is on-brand and that you wouldn't mind others seeing the source of that repost.

81
Video Snippets & Teasers

Video snippets are short preview videos. Video snippets are good promotional material because they draw social media viewers directly to your video and encourage them to watch the full version. This is easy to do using a platform like Instagram TV (IGTV). If you post a video using IGTV, you can also cross-post on Facebook and create a snippet all at one time. (See Instagram.com) Even if you decide to go 100% YouTube for all of your full videos, providing a snippet or shorter version of the video on another platform will attract more viewers to your video platform and yield more Shine Online by growing your viewership.

82
Questions, Actions, & Polls

Questions, actions and polls are all interactive pieces of content that engage your online audience by asking them to do something. For example, YouTuber and social media influencer, Ralph Smart's Instagram profile includes posts that ask the audience to take action and agree with his inspirational posts by saying "Yes" quite often. All social media users are now able to easily post content in their Instagram stories including polls, countdowns, questions/ answers and other calls to action. These posts help you shine on social media by engaging the audience. People love to be engaged and it allows them to remember their experiences. Thus, when you create interactive posts, you are providing your audience with a unique user experience that they can remember and enjoy. And since people always come back for experiences that they enjoy, actionable posts that are highly engaging will keep those followers coming back to see what's next.

83
Upcoming Events & Event Recaps

Shine on social media by posting about events of interest to your audience. Events are collective gatherings and your online audience might be seeking to have real social contact offline. Posting about your upcoming events will attract interest online. Be sure to communicate important information about your events including purpose, date, time and place. Simple enough, but on social media we tend to forget what might be common when we are using another media like traditional invitations. Attending certain events can also help to build your personal brand by showing your interest and hobbies.

One great tactic that I've seen used well on social media is posting videos and photos of past events in order to attract newcomers. This strategy shows the power of multimedia, connecting ideas with video and using social media as a mass exhibition channel. You can also connect with other users at an event if you want to easily expand your brand. This is important because after (or during) the event, you can post content and tag users you connected with, which means you will become connected to their audience through tagging and sharing. If you host your own event or attend one, take great photos to capture the moments and scenery that will make content posting easy later.

Bright Ideas: Here are some ideas to improve your content from events

ï Look for event banners or posters and take photos by them.

ï Find a tribe and get their social media handles for tagging.

ï Tag the location if you want it referenced in your post (this can be general, like the city you are in).

84
Special Interest: Fashion, Modeling, Clothing, Accessories

Social media is a primary medium for posting stylish fashion whether on the runway or at a red-carpet premiere, celebrity fashion trends make waves online. Posting about fashion on mainstream social media is hugely valuable as seen by Instagram's current 700 million-plus hashtags about #Fashion. Fashion influencers and brands have leveraged social media's visual display qualities to expand the fashion industry itself online. Social media posts about fashion can include posts of actual clothing, online boutiques, models, and bloggers, to name a few common ways fashion is featured online. Fashion on social media is great for displaying products, attracting niche audiences and producing great sales.

Even if your brand is not selling fashion directly, many users make money from modeling clothing online and becoming brand ambassadors on social media. The key to remember here is that fashion sells and gains a great deal of shine on social media when displayed well. Thus, the best way to display fashion content is via quality photos and videos.

Keep in mind that celebrities selling fashion clearly have a greater advantage online because they already have massive audiences and a faithful following of fans. So, you shouldn't expect to have the same sales as Khloe Kardashian's 'Good American' brand overnight. However, success is still possible because fashion is a large market with room for the growth for new brands. To build their following, a fashion newcomer will have to post more content with value and connect with influencers that will share their brand with new audiences online. Shine on social media by displaying your high-quality fashion, even if it is just for a special day, users like when you like your confidence in what you and you will shine in your photos.

Utilizing my background in modeling and acting, I learned to shine in the area of fashion on my Instagram account by regularly blogging about my style. My fashion posts became some of my most popular posts analytically and engagement wise. I also learned how to monetize my social media through fashion by becoming a fashion affiliate and influencer. As a fashion influencer, I created creative posts to celebrate the fashion brands that I affiliated with. I quickly gained high levels of engagement online from brands and followers alike, which helped my social media growth and Shine Online, however there are many other ways to blog about fashion and make money online. You can become a fashion influencer by having a style blog that talks about celebrity and street style fashion or by becoming a stylist and selling product. Show off your own unique fashion style to grow your influence on social media and join the constant conversation about fashion to Shine Online with style.

85
Special Interest: Health & Fitness

Health as a special interest is an extremely popular subject on social media. Influencers post their health routines regularly and often gain clients in the area of nutrition, fitness or other wellness-related subjects including mental health. On Instagram.com the hashtag, # fitness, currently has over 360 million posts on Instagram alone. There are many subsets of fitness including yoga in this massive content idea. The key to shining social media pages on health to find a specific fitness idea and post about it consistently. In addition, connect with people you've helped to build continued support and brand loyalty. Fitness as a content idea will always Shine Online as many people are seeking self-improvement ideas online.

86
Special Interest: Technology

Technology is a constantly growing field with a broad spectrum of new products, ideas, training and innovative devices. Online posts about technology can include product reviews, actual products, new technology, or helpful apps that people many find useful online. When you post about technology online, your content will be about what value the particular technology offers the user. Tech value can also include training on use of any technology including more practical technology like digital camera use or more complex ideas like coding for websites. The goal with posting about technology is to find a niche audience and speak to them consistently. When it comes to technology, it is important to speak in a mainstream way that the audience can understand and navigate. Remember, if you use technical lingo and acronyms your audience is not familiar with, your audience could get lost and not understand you, so be specific and profile definitions if needed. When posting about a tech product, high-quality media displaying its use is helpful. Shine through your knowledge of tech or your amazing product, just make sure it adds value and others can connect with it.

87
Special Interest:
Beauty and Makeup Products

Makeup and beauty is currently a billion-dollar business with multi-millionaires like Kylie Jenner influencing the industry in new ways via social media. Kylie began as a television co-star with her older sisters, the Kardashians. Next, she began a blog as a teen and started modeling. Next, even with a bit of controversy, her social media following took off. With social media as her primary medium of exhibition, she displayed her lips in an appealing way online, via high-quality photography. The next step would be... well, the million-dollar leap. Jenner launched her make-up line, Kylie Lip Kits, in which she promoted on social media via photos and quality content, letting her audience know what was coming next. The result was a sold-out product that even crashed her sales website! Needless to say, business was booming. Kylie utilized her controversy, passion and look to amplify her social media and sell beauty products online. Now, her friends and siblings have special makeup lines in connection with her line, like Kim X Kylie, where she utilizes her sister's popular influencer brands along with her product to boost sales across the board.

Now, how does that apply to you? You are likely not a TV reality star, but the goal here is to look at a product like beauty, something that you love and grow using a passionate perspective. Let your social media audience know why you are passionate about beauty and why you love your product. Next, display it in such a way that your followers can get an idea of the product, why it is unique and how it can help them solve a problem. Please note understanding the solution your specific production brings is very important when customers have many options of places to buy. I have seen start- up brands with no brand identity and they suffer greatly, so take time to think about how your brand can help someone. Show you passion for your brand consistently and your product or idea will Shine Online. Again, don't forget the power of influence. Collaborate with beauty and makeup influencers and your brand will expand by having a larger reach for potential sales.

88
Promotional Content Posts

Promotions are online content presented to encourage your audience to take action, whether it be to buy something that you never knew you wanted or to register for something. The best promotions speak to the audience by first being appealing to the eye. Next, they should first contain promotional content, text and graphic, that speak to your audience. If you are not a natural writer or public relations guru, you should hire one to help you create and curate promotional content. The next step is that your promotional post should have easy access for follow up action, which could be clicking a link, following your page or another action that your promotion is seeking. Promotions are great content, but they should be used in combination with a social media marketing strategy that combines your valuable content with an opportunity.

#PromoContent

For example, many coaches now use Instagram as a primary mode of recruiting clients. They post an interesting visual or video and explain in their captions the significance of their promoted content. They might go over their professional experience and how it could help their clients. These promotions typically have a link saying something like: "Learn More."

I utilize my background in media, writing, and PR to often create my own social media promotions myself. However, I like to get a fresh perspective to see if my content is reaching my audience by listening to my audience to see if my promotions are effective. One way to listen to your audience is by seeing if they engage with your promotional content. You can then began to understand if a change is needed and start using social media strategies, including those in this book, to implement new strategies for your promotional content.

For assistance creating shining promotional content online follow my Instagram @LearnMediaToday or reach out at www.learnmediatoday.com for resources.

89
Entertainment Posts

Entertainment content is fun, light and enjoyable for users to watch and engage in. Entertainment content on social media can come in many forms including short series, comedy, and live shows, to name a few options. Entertainment content is as limitless as the creative concepts that one can create. For example, the rise of entertainment video memes occurred simultaneously with the rise of the popular app, Vine, which featured micro video posts. These short videos were used as the optimum entertainment pieces on social media because they were short, to the point and often hilarious.

To create entertainment content, you should decide on a theme and what medium that you want to present it in. Video entertainment is popular on social media and can build a following. To be great, like @kingbach, consistency and fresh ideas are a must. Also, using hashtags like #comedyposts might also help you gain traction on social media. Shine Online by bringing your unique entertainment content and encourage your audience to like and follow your brand to continue to build a following.

90
Artistic Posts

If you have a passion for the arts or you can build a following based on your art, you should be posting about it. Many artists are famous on social media for posting their artwork featuring celebrities online. Since apps like Instagram primarily feature photos and visuals, there are ample opportunities to display you work and also let your audience know what inspires you. Placing your information or a link on your Instagram or Facebook biography will also help your followers to learn more and be encouraged to purchase your work.

If you are not an artist, sometimes a creative post of art that inspires you can also attract attention to your profile. For example, Atlanta's Living Walls, or graffiti walls, are now popular tourist attractions in Atlanta, GA. The large colorful murals make perfect photo opportunities for those that embrace them by taking Instagram worthy shots in front of them. Shine Online by celebrating art or finding a beautiful wall to tastefully show off.

91
Post About Your Business Services

When you represent your business on social media you are taking a leap of faith, so it must be activated thoughtfully and with professionalism. Thus, you must ensure that branding and public relations are considered at all times when posting content about your business and services. Business and service posts can include a list of services available and other valuable visuals to help your audience learn about your business. If you post about business services, it is best to have samples of you performing that service as you build clients over time. Be clear about your business goals and purpose to make your posts Shine Online. Also, refer to strategies #11 on Call to Action, #88 Promotional Content Posts, and the last chapter on social media monetization for more about how to promote business content on social media.

92
Behind the Scenes Photos (BTS)

One interesting way to post content about your business or brand that will engage audiences is to post behind the scenes video or photos of you doing your business. For example, a start-up founder could post a video of the process of interviewing a long line of potential hires for their business or post a creative photo about it, letting the audience know of their growing success.

Are you a photographer? You could have a friend or partner take photos of you in action during a shoot to show off your professional talents. While working as a photographer/media producer, I realized that my audience needed to see me in action creating media to become more supportive of me and what I could do. So, I had a friend help me with a photoshoot by taking photos of me taking photos. On another instance, I was producing a major media project, a TV pilot, with so many moving parts, I had no time to think of taking behind the scenes photos. Having someone do it for me turned out to be an outstanding add to my social media, not to mention it is great archival media to look back on. One   of my most "liked" photos on Instagram was one of me working on a production in heels, holding a stack of papers and directing my production crew. Clearly, the sky's the limit when it comes   to behind the scenes content because there are so many creative ways to express your overall experience behind the curated brand. One thing for sure, is that BTS content engages audiences because the audience feels like they are a part of what you are doing. That engagement is important when building brand loyalty, interest, likes and Shining Online.

#BehindTheScenes

Sunshine West behind the scenes, on-set of her 20-West Entertainment Company TV pilot production "Dance Street ATL".

There are as many paths to creating shining unique content as there are creative users on social media. The important factor to remember is to be on-brand while also being authentic and spontaneous or creative when the time is right. Bring positive posts to your social media and engage with others whom pages that you admire. Shine Online via posting your own content that shines, that is content you are passionate about, proud of and that connects with your audience.

Chapter 6

Strategic Ways to Make Money Online: Creating Profit from your Platform

Would you like to make money starting by just having access to a social media account? Perhaps you have little to no marketing or technical experience and think it's not possible. Well, it is. You are now becoming informed and this is the right place for you to start your journey, not just building influence by Shining Online, but profiting financially from your platforms.

In this section, we will discuss strategies to profit from your platform. Each strategy will take time to hone and may or may not yield profits overnight. It is up to you as the brand strategist for your own social media or brand to make things happen or get assistance with each process you embrace. The great thing about social media is that there will always be changes and room from growth. If one platform or monetization method does not work for you, try another until you reach your goals. You will ultimately reach your goals through practice, strategies, platform mastery and consistency. Using the methods below, you can expect to generate leads the first time around using monetization methods, and with consistency and refinement of your practices, your profit will grow. Learning is the first step, taking action is next, so review the guidelines below for information on how to start monetizing your social media today.

Remember, monetizing is a fancy word for making money by

converting social content into profit. You can do it. Embrace your authentic brand and tell people what you have to offer. It's time to live the dream, end procrastinating and make money online. Here are the strategies to profit from your platform.

Please visit Instagram @LearnMediaToday and www. LearnMediaToday.com for more information on business strategies, live training and coaching or reach out directly at www. sunshinewest.org, my coaching website.

93
Build Click Funnels $$$

Click funnels make it easy for your audience to come to you and buy your service on social media, blogs and associated websites. If you have a service or product, it is important to have user-friendly functions, and that's where click or sales funnels come in. These are systems input into your social media, websites or blogs that make it easy for your audience to click and purchase your service. Sometimes the top of the funnel starts with a registration with your audience's emails, however the "end game" is to lead them to a sale.

The social media analytics website, **crazyegg.com,** describes the sales or click funnels using the acronym AIDA: awareness, interest, decision, action. In this case, building awareness is at the top of the funnel. The awareness component includes any activity that you do to draw in a lead online. Thus, the strategies in this book that include posting blogs, microblogs, Facebook Ads or Tweets, are examples of ways to raise awareness of your information, when your audience clicks on captivating content that they deem useful.

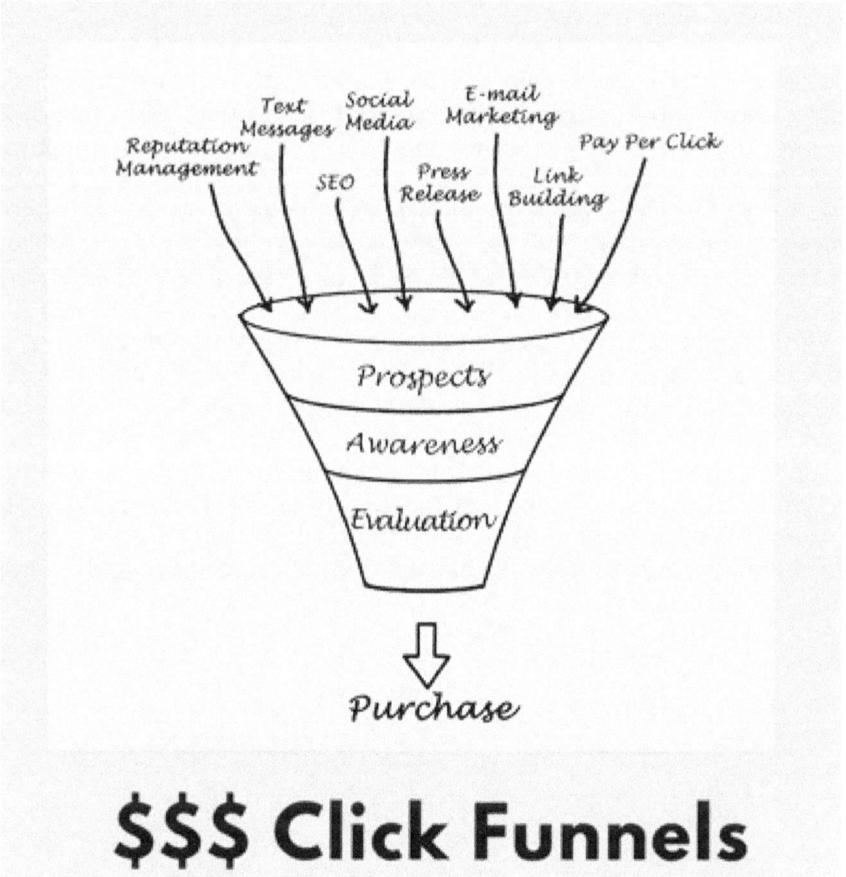

The second step in a typical funnel is interest, however interest is built into the sales funnel lead capture page itself. The page that can generate interest is one of the master conversion points because, "if you're…posting interesting content, and your followers are aware of what your business does, followers can become customers (John, 2018)." Can you get your customers' email or a "like" in exchange for some valuable content (Mulvey, 2018)? This should be the minimal goal of your sales funnel page. The emails are leads and this part of the process is also lead generation because you will be obtaining information and direct contact with those interested in what you have to offer. The great thing about leads at this point is that by the time they have offered their emails, they have already patronized and shown interest in your product through reviewing your free valuable content.

The next step, the decision, is often made after a consumer   of your sales funnel page reviews valuable content and decides whether to buy in or not. You can reasonably conclude if no one buys in or registers, that you need improvements in your product or your sales tactic. Find help through analytical data evaluations or through simply asking users, friends, or brand strategist how your content is coming across. Using strategies in this book effectively is a start.

The last piece of action depends on the sales funnel where the ultimate action is to make the decision to buy what your selling, whether it's information, a service, or a simple product.

While online, you may have stumbled upon training that you can't live without because there is so much convincing information that you are itching to press "BUY" at the end of the page. In this case, you have reached a sales funnel page with items of interest and value.

In order to get a click funnel, one must set it up with a developer or develop one yourself. Websites like clickfunnels.com or smaller boutique funnel websites are great ways to start if you want assistance with creating a click funnel. However, there are platforms and websites now that make this simple for you to do. Teachable. com allows course creators to create their own funnel sales type page. This page is complete with the school name, course title, room for testimonials, instructor bio and much more, with the final touch of a place for customers to say "yes!" and buy in.

Sales funnels are amazing fairly new ways of generating leads and making money online. Through your brand's product and sales tactics, you can achieve much financial success when consumers/ users buy-in; however, the rule of authenticity remains. People do not, I repeat, do not, need you to be famous to buy-in, but they do need you to have what they are looking for. That's why the funnel is important, so be sure your awareness is on-point with a clear idea about what you offer and why you are "the one" to buy from in the era of digital offer crowding. How do you stand out? Be sure your audience knows and can clearly see how you can help them. **#GenerateLeads**

94
Blogs with Ad Banners and Links

 Are Word Press type blogs Social Media? No, but it's one of the strongest links we can have to social media, in fact, many social media outlets like Instagram are actually considered a type of blog. Nowadays, it doesn't have to be Word Press to be a blog, it just has to be a consistent online posting, with a purpose, about a topic.

Blogs! Blogs! Blogs! We see them everywhere, all day, and you know what? They work! According to the blog information and statistics website, bloggingbasics101.com, 77% of Internet users read blogs. In addition, the site notes that blogging is great for business because blogs help generate 126% leads for small businesses, with 61% of consumers making a purchase because of a blog.

But how? And more importantly, why? The method of how is somewhat simple. Today's blogging website builders have built- in features like the ability to add links to a blog, which allows for monetization. When you share another brand's link in your blog, you are advertising their business and they can pay you for your endorsement of their business, especially if a purchase is made. To take it further, post advertising banners to your blog and get paid for cost per click (CPC) advertising. You get paid for clicks on those posted banners, which leads consumers to the brand being advertised. Another method to monetize is to work with an online advertising program like Google AdSense, which adds advertising banners to your blog to help you generate profit through the placement of the ads. A blog can also be an instrumental method to generate leads with an attached sales funnel, which is discussed in strategy #92.

Generating money from blogs is marathon process, it takes time to build and gain a following. The first step is to choose a topic that you are passionate about or have interest in and start creating valuable content. Then you must learn how to translate the value to dollars either via including ads or another means, such as selling a product. Always ensure your content is relatable for the audience that you hope to attract.

Bright Ideas for Blogging: Blog monetization takes time and likely a cross-platform effort. This means you don't want to just rely on your awesome writing but aim to integrate your blog with other social media like Facebook, Twitter, Pinterest or Instagram to draw in the crowds to your blog. Provide a link to your blog on your non- blog social media networks. Also, have sneak peeks on social media to show people your blog is worth reading online. Write your blog, but don't stop there, know you can expand from the basic platform to profiting by promoting your brand through this medium. A great blog idea also helps when drawing in the crowd. Ask yourself if you would want to read it. If yes, so will your core audience. #Write

Use this guidebook for help on strategies to add value and specialized content ideas for your blog or reach out to @LearnMediaToday for tools or coaching for your blog.

95
Blog as an Affiliate Influencer

Blog Affiliate Programs

There are many ways to make money from blogging and micro blogging, but one of the most popular ways includes adding links to endorse a product via becoming an product affiliate or influencer. Affiliate bloggers and influencers have an agreement to receive commissions, payments or free products in exchange for posting about a brand's product or service. It is kind of like writing an article endorsing a product, like a commercial, in exchange for money or goods, most of the time money. This method works; however, from the start, make sure the agreement is clear on whether you are going to be paid in money or goods and be informed of *when* you will be paid. Successful affiliate bloggers who represent brands exceptionally well are sought after by additional brands who want you to represent their brand.

Personally, after becoming an affiliate for one popular fashion brand and posting only on Instagram, over 18 companies contacted me to become an affiliate for their brands. Be aware that even though you'll earn a commission, some of these companies want you to purchase their products at a discount. This works great in the fashion blogger world. However, I've seen blogs advertising anything from cleaning products to hygiene products, showing that any brand will use an affiliated blogger to help them market and sell their product. It is up to you to find the best deals and highest-paying brands that will help you to monetize your blog. Of course, the higher the traffic on your blog, the larger the opportunity for you.

Bloggers who act as affilate partners for a brand gain money online when someone buys a product that they promote.

Your social media blog does not have to have only full of affiliate ads to monetize, but making a profit depends on how much you are willing to advertise on your blog. Some users may feel that adding advertisements or links takes away from their authenticity. However, the important thing to remember is to *remain* authentic and only advertise what you know is a good product or idea worthy of writing about and attaching yourself to. You will certainly Shine Online as your audience looks to see which exciting brands you affiliate with making money through affiliate marketing is the like icing on the cake.

96
Selling Products Online, E-Commerce

Selling products online, as in e-commerce, is one major way to make money online using social media. Direct sales are becoming increasingly popular using social media platforms. I remember in the early days of Instagram, around 2013, I had a private account. Some of the top people requesting to follow me where online fashion boutiques. Initially, it felt annoying! However, now I realize this was a marketing tool to get me in front of their online brand. Now, the e-commerce industry has taken off on social media. Just think, shopify.com says that Instagram has over 1 billion active users. So, why not sell to them outside of your main website?

Right now, selling on social media, especially Instagram, is more user-friendly and functional than ever. In the early days of Instagram and Facebook, the most an online store could do is provide a link to a sales page while promoting their products online. Now brands using Facebook to promote their businesses can have a store using Shopify directly on their Facebook pages. Instagram store pages have long had a space for placing links to a business online store, but now stores can actually add special shopping tags on their product photos on Instagram that will lead users directly to a purchase page. The ease of use of these new social e-commerce tools and the advancement in the e-commerce technology make it more beneficial now, than ever, for e-commerce brands to sell on social media. This is because buyers won't have many steps to click through (often 1) to get to a point of sale and that makes it easier for brands to sell to speedily to buyers online. Social media as an e-commerce tool is a must and staying up to date on the newest retail technologies is what will provide the purchasing edge you need to succeed. To make your store Shine Online review the specialized content ideas #84 and #87 in this book.

Check out an article on shopping on Instagram to help you build an active and effective Instagram shop at https://www.shopify.com/blog/instagram-shopping

97
Use Paid Advertisements & Sponsored Promotions

Paid advertisements make it easier to make money online by allowing you to increase your reach and promote your brand directly to consumers. Instagram and Facebook allow the use and creation of targeted advertisements, also called promotions. Advertisements lead to sales because your audience has easy access through promoted posts online, when the platform exposes your post to larger audiences. Promoted posts do not have to be expensive, but in order to be effective they should last at least three days. If you are just trying to gain likes, one day may suffice, but if your goal is to maximize your earnings online, you'll want to run a longer promotion. The advantage of a promoted post is that you can identify and target your audience to reach the core audience that you want to sell to. On Instagram and Facebook uses are able to decide on how many people that they want their Ad to reach. The more you pay for the Ad, the further, in numbers, it will reach to audiences online.

Targeting & Placement ✎ Edit

Location:
United States

Interests: **Social media**

Excluded Connections:
Pages
Exclude people who like Buffer

Age: **18 - 65+**

Language: **English (US)**

Mobile Placement: **News Feed**

Desktop: **News Feed or Right Column**

Estimated Daily Reach

1,200 - 3,200 people

0   of 14,000,000

This is only an estimate. Numbers shown are based on the average performance of ads targeted to your selected audience.

Example of Facebook Ad Targeting

Your brand's promoted post should include a quality photo, convincing story and a call to action. To optimize your promotion, add a video or spend a bit more in order for your post to be shared with a broader audience.

Currently on Facebook and Instagram, a business account is required for a promoted post. With a reported 3.48 billion users of social media as of early 2019, per thenextweb.com, surely there are a few million shopping online. In fact, per Statista, 2.8 billion people around the world now shop online. Increasing your reach with a promotion is not only smart, it is a must-do in order to compete when you are ready to build increased revenue off an established brand. Make sure your posts are non-offensive or they won't be approved by the platform. Also ensure ease of use and tell your audience exactly what to do with no confusion. Before you know it, you will rack up social media likes and high levels of interest that lead to purchasing action using your social media ads.

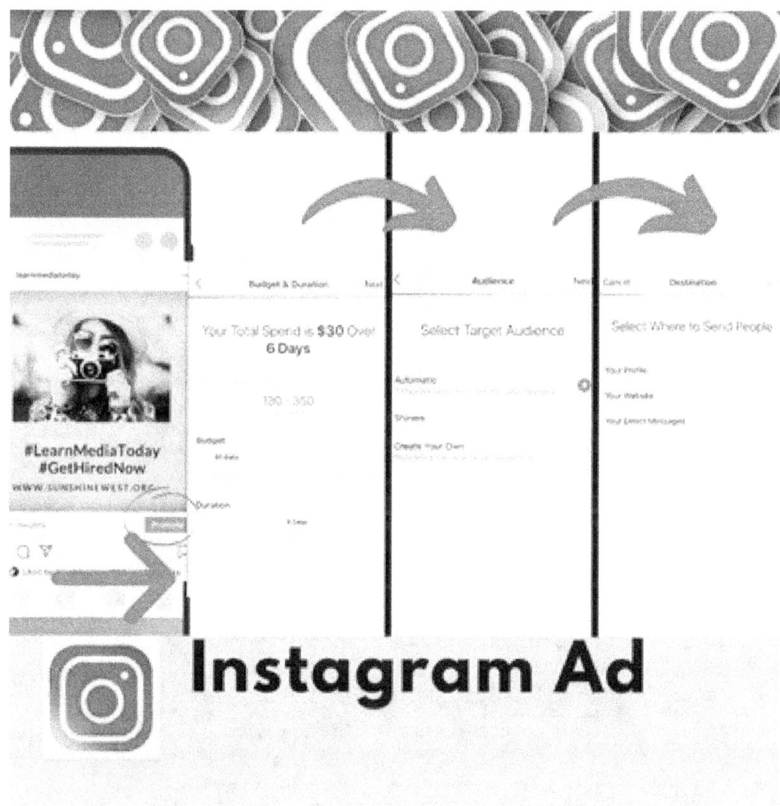

98
Create Digital Education and Information Products

The sale of online information products via social media lead generation is a market that is hot right now. Per Statista, the digital education market is expected to produce over 243 billion U.S. dollars by 2022. Information product industry includes digital courses, instructional design, e-books and other e-learning modes including webinars.

Although this online education market has been around for a while, it is still an emerging market with high potential. Unlike selling retail, gaining traction in this industry will require you to build a significant level of influence, even while you market the course itself. This means if you don't have a large following, you will need more promoted posts to sell your digital information product. If you have a large following, you will need to transition your entertainment value on social media into a tangible product for your audience, which will take work from you offline. The work includes writing and designing your information product. This includes creating video, book or e-book or presentations. The next step is marketing. Your edge is that you are likely an expert in this space, thus you should know where to find the audience that will need your product. This is helpful when developing an information product because your very niche audience will want to learn your specific information because the product will serve them well.

Get help creating an information product by reviewing Teachable. com or Udemy for ideas on courses. Or take an online course yourself to get a flow of how it all works. You are bound to learn something new to help your information product shine on social media.

Bright Ideas: So, you know your industry and what you want to sell an information product based around it. That's a start. You build a course, but the hardest part is getting people to press the "buy now" button. Or is it? Currently, there are many courses on how to become an online course creator that are very valuable if you want to improve your skills in marketing a course. If this is an area of struggle, find a course creation consultant, online marketing consultant or business model that can help you.

99
Create a Podcast Series

Linking your social media following to a podcast can mean big bucks for you from advertisements and other monetary sources. Podcasts are digital radio broadcasts, though not considered social media, they are considered a type of new media and can be linked to your social media following. Podcasting can present you as authority within your field and are a great place for you to send your social media followers to begin to monetize your brand.

How are podcasts monetized?

Advertisements: One way to make money podcasting is through gaining paid sponsorships. Advertisers place their commercials on your podcast and in exchange, you are paid according to how many people download your podcast. Under the CPM model (cost per impression), podcasters are paid for every 1000 downloads. The amount you get paid varies depending on how long the ads are. So, for a one-minute ad, you are getting paid more than you would for a 15-second promotion.

Affiliate Partnerships: In addition, affiliate marketing is another way to monetize your podcast. Mentioning products or services that help you can mean big bucks in the long term. To do this, develop a partnership with a brand as an affiliate marketer. Find a partnership by asking brands if they use affiliates or by joining an affiliate program that exists on a brand's website.

Selling Products: Selling your own products on podcasts can start with a simple mention. The best way to do this is to have a website, which could also be the one you use for your podcast, that you can refer people to for your product. Quality content and building a following by selling products through your podcast along with social media will bring monetary success.

Interviewing & Collaborating: Interviewing and collaborating are the true power in podcasts. Why? Because like social media, whomever you interview (preferably someone with a following) will promote your episode because they are on it, which leads to growing your podcast. In addition, interviewing provides amazing content that listeners can listen to again and again.

Bright Ideas: How to Start? If you want to try podcasting, you can easily start from home. You will need a good quality microphone, a quiet recording area and great subjects to talk about aka *content*. Get your podcast active on iTunes by recording at least three podcasts and then submit it for approval — and like magic — you are now a podcaster! Remember to promote your podcast on social media to build your Shine Online and growth. One interesting way to share your accomplishment of becoming a podcaster on social media by providing teasers of your podcast.

100
Grow Your Following & Influence

Growth always means change and growing your influence online is no different. Growing your influence via the strategies in this book, in addition to emerging strategies will increase your following and influence. Consistency with posting combined with an interesting brand with an authentic voice will sustain your growth. To grow your influence, adapt a handful of the strategies mentioned in this book and cater them to your brand.

In terms of content, your posts should, without question, be geared at your target audience. You can obtain information about your target audience by using analytics websites to research whom your industry serves and what they respond to online.

To measure success, review the responsiveness of online users to understand the effectiveness of your social media posts. In addition, review the demographics behind who responds to your posts to measure the overall effectiveness of your posts. Are you driving traffic? Are you gaining leads? Are your leads converting? They will. Just stay in the influencing arena by not giving up and you will see the responsiveness that you need from those that need your services or products. The Internet, particularly social media, is highly competitive, thus, if you want to stand out and grow, you must again, be consistent and produce quality media content.

Remember that the art of influence is the art of engaging and inspiring through a mediated format. Thankfully, multiple platforms are at your fingertips to help you inspire and influence. If you are not a fashion or beauty blogger, yes, there is still a place for you. Many hard news and socially conscious influencers utilize Twitter as their main platform. Regardless of the platform(s) you choose
ñ YouTube, SnapChat, Twitter, and/or Instagram – leverage each

platform's strength to gain traction in the form of followers and influence. Later, monetize by presenting yourself as an influencer or expert of your brand. Influencer-based monetization occurs through selling merchandise, coaching or providing other services related to your influence. Grow loyalty in order to grow monetarily.

Bright Ideas: If you don't grow through social influence in a monetary way, you must ask, who are the customers? And how can I bring my message to them with a presentation worthy of a sale, both on and offline? Remember your social media can be an anchor for your business by displaying what you can do, but you must drive forward your business efforts for more than just likes! For example, if you are a food influencer/private chef, display your process and why your clients satisfied with your work, while your actual business takes place offline, the interesting behind the scenes display will draw in new customers. Clear brand representation on social media will impact your sales. To build influence be sure that your posts support your brand an elicit customer response. Gain loyalty and growth by reaching out to your audience, providing value online or inspiring them.

Bright Ideas 2: Build success as an Influencer by asking these questions.

- Who is my core audience?

- What are their interests?

- How can I serve their interest?

- What do they need and want?

- How can my brand solve a problem using my talent, knowledge and skills?

- What needs to be on my social media in order build influence in this area?

- What other brands can I affiliate or partner with to grow my brand?

101
Create Your YouTube Channel

YouTube is a form of new media in which users are able to create original videos for broadcast online to a wide range of users worldwide. Imagine, anybody with an email can create a YouTube account (that's a lot of people!). The reach of YouTube is undeniable with its two billion logged-in monthly users per statista. com. YouTube, which began in 2005, has grown tremendously from what it was originally considered: a fun video platform. Now, YouTube is a giant platform with a variety of content from corporate videos, to instructional, to, of course, entertainment and comedy.

YouTube is also a full-time job and wealth builder for those that use it best. So, how can you leverage the platform to create or grow your business? Well, the magic is as simple as 1, 2, 3. Post a few great videos, get viewers and start building a following. The good news is that anyone can post a video and original content, giving them a chance to grow their brand. The harsh news is that YouTube is currently only allowing accounts with 4000 watched hours and 1000 subscribers, all gained within a year, to receive a portion of their ad revenue through the YouTube Partner Program (YPP) per youtube.com (YouTube.com, n.d.). Is this an issue? Not really, every business starts from the ground up, but while you are building your viewers, there are still a few valuable things you can do to start making money through the platform immediately.

Making Money on YouTube With or Without Subscribers:

- **YouTube Partnership Program (YPP):** With the YouTube Partnership Program you must gain subscribers and join the program, described above and on youtube.com.

- **Plug your Biz:** Pitch your business in your videos to by posting videos that lead clients to your service: cooking, writing, organizing, etc.

- **Merch Sales:** Sell merchandise through YouTube by displaying it or telling people the value of your product in a video.

- **Superchat:** Host live video with YouTube's Superchat. This is another element that you must get approved to do. Yet, if approved, you will be able to host live video sessions and receive monetary payments from users during your chat (YouTube.com, n.d.).

- **Build Partnerships:** Partnerships with other brands can mean big bucks. You can present products on your YouTube channel videos and earn money from another brand. This includes product placement and any other partnerships you may form. It is a simple method; however, the content must be worthy for a brand to work with you, yet you might be surprised how many might want to work with you if you are reaching their target audience. This is a major way that I see people benefit on YouTube platforms. One way to go this path to monetization is by becoming an influencer in a specific area. Brands will want to partner with you when they know that you have a target audience that you can reach through your videos.

- **Channel Memberships:** Channel Memberships are private groups on YouTube where members pay for exclusive content. This is great when you have a loyal following because membership payments are consistent income. You will need to keep interest in your group to keep new members coming in and to prevent membership loss or turnover (YouTube.com, n.d.).

- **Cross Social Media Promotion:** This is a bit about marketing. So, you ask yourself despite having 1,000 Instagram followers and tons of views, why is your channel struggling? The answer is that you are not cross marketing.

When you feel stunted on YouTube, there are two major

strategic marketing strategies that you can implement. First, as discussed, use **cross platform promoting: Cross** promoting on other social media platforms about your YouTube channel will allow all of your followers to know about your YouTube channel and seek out the content if it is of value to them.

Secondly, remember that you can target your audience through paid ads. Make sure you are reaching your target audience with your ad content, even across platforms. So, if you post about your new channel on Facebook, you can also target your audience through hashtags or even paid advertisements on Facebook. Using paid advertisements will help you direct your content to your desired target audience and start drawing people to your platform and purpose.

YouTube is not an automatic cash cow. You have to put in the work creating many videos with great content that interests your audience first. While learning to create video content for YouTube, you are likely to experience some trial and error learning to light, edit and set design for your video. However, if you like media, that's the fun part!

Here are quick tips for having a successful YouTube channel:

1. **Produce valuable content:** Create content your audience needs or is entertained by; this will keep them coming back for more views.

2. **Produce a Quality Product:** Your video quality is likely to change over time for the better, but a few critical requirements must be met for a video to be considered quality for posting. Those include adequate lighting and a good camera that presents clear visuals as discussed in the Strategic Media Tools section of this book. Your lighting can be daylight from a window --- as long as your audience can see you well.

V once watched a YouTube video about a woman who talked about saving money on her channel. She was not lit very well in her video because all of her lights were off during the daytime in her video- why? Well, it was one of her methods! Odd, but entertaining and informative. I could see her with her window open, so it worked. As far as cameras go, yes, a cell phone with a quality video recording system will work. Now there are no reasons why you can't make a video because supplies are less expensive and easier to find.

1. **Post Consistently:** Provide consistency with posting your video content. This means that you don't post once every three months. One per week is sufficient to start. Popular YouTubers like Gillian Perkins posts two videos per week and lets her audience know when they will drop or be posted. Allowing your audience to know your post schedule can help you gain immediate views as people will be expecting your post on a certain day or time.

However, if you "tube" on YouTube, pun intended, you should enjoy what you are bringing to the table. Your audience may be able to tell if you do not care about what you are posting, so build your brand using authenticity by caring about, enjoying or knowing a lot about your subject matter. Ultimately, when you put your all into creating quality videos with valuable content, you will yield major profits and successes both on and off the platform because people will be getting to know you directly, even from your own home.

As you grow in influence you can decide which business method you want to adopt to monetize your YouTube channel. If you are only having fun making videos for a while, that's ok too. You can Shine Online with YouTube, see what you subscribers are interested in, and take your business ideas from there. Use YouTube for monetization as you build your influence.

Bright Ideas: Keep them Watching – Utilize the "watch next" feature to keep your audience watching. The website will allow you to add a bubble to your videos that will notify users of a video title they can watch next. That feature keeps interested users engaged and watching.

Conclusion

Shine On, You Can Build A Brand &Following

Ok, so now you have read 101 Ways to Shine Online, with 101 social media strategies for engaging content, monetization, creative content ideas and growth on social media. So what's next? How do you start? Now is the time to start your journey Shining Online by implementing strategies that help you change your world and online brand for the better.

Start by understanding yourself, your brand and how it can serve others. Then move forward strategically, Shining Online: collaborate, connect and most importantly, listen to your followers. Display content ideas on your social media based on the strategies and ideas in this book or connect them to emerging ones. Call your community to inspired action and grow your influence through consistency. Build your brand using the Shine Online Strategy Building Method featured in the section, "How to Use This Book." Most importantly, understand that what you put out online influences not just your 'page' and followers, but the world at large. You are influencing and creating. You are shining.

The content and monetization strategies in this book are not simply made up to make you feel better about your social media page. Either, I have tried the strategies myself and saw positive analytical results or researched successful social media pages and textual research to bring you this valuable information. When I began to brand myself on social media, within a month I became an influencer and went from 13 Instagram story views per day to about 500 hundred or so viewers within less than a day. I was surprised by my swift growth on social media. But it had 100% to do with creative content, increased engagement and monetization strategies. They are here, in this book. Use them to Shine Online.

Lastly, please remember, I am here for you as a media and career coach. I will help you to create creative original ideas for your brand

and offer more strategic ways that you can improve your brand using my knowledge of social media, business marketing, graphics and branding. I provide services in career coaching, social media marketing, business marketing and media training. I am here for every bright, inspired reader and customer of this book. Please reach out for coaching, training or an easy online training session to improve your brand.

Visit Instagram @LearnMediaToday and @ShineOnline.Book to join our community and to start a conversation about media. Also for training visit www.LearnMediaToday.com for more information on business strategies, webinars and coaching or reach out directly at www.sunshinewest.org , my coaching website.

*Book Reader Bonus Tool: For New Instagram Algorithm Hacks -Visit and Follow @LearnMediaToday and subscribe to www.SunshineWest.org

Shine Online Glossary

Strategic, Emerging, and Innovative practices (S.E.I) – Adopting S.E.I. means to adopt emerging media in a strategic way as an act of innovation.

Social Media – Social media is both Internet and mobile based content presented to users via websites and mobile apps that are used for collaboration, engagement and direct response from users to users and audience to creator in support of a given topic or idea.

Shine Online – Shining online is the act of gaining both visual success in the form of engagement and analytic success while using social media to brand yourself online. To Shine Online means to gain desired success that helps you build a brand and following.

Era of Influence - The era or unique time period which embraces influence culture on social media, further defining the culture of the time period.

Voice of Influence. (V.O.I) – original voice of social media content creator that acts as an authority to influence on a topic featured on social media.

Super Follower – A follower that is loyal due to high level of interest in your brand through a process of qualifying through content appreciation and active engagement.

Sunshine's Golden Rule- Be good at being your best self, become authentic by identifying factors that make you unique and boosting them to build your brand.

Book References

Lua, A. (2019, January 24). 21 Top Social Media Sites to Consider for Your Brand -. Retrieved March 07, 2020, from https://buffer.com/library/social-media-sites

YouTube.com (n.d.). Engaging with fans through Super Chat and Super Stickers. Retrieved March 07, 2020, from https://creatoracademy.youtube.com/page/lesson/superchat?hl=en

Kerpen, D., Rosenbluth, M., & Riedinger, M. (2015). Likeable social media: How to delight your customers, create an irresistible brand, and be amazing on facebook, twitter, linkedln, instagram, pinterest, and more. New York, NY: McGraw-Hill Education.

Quicksprout.com. (2019, January 4). The Complete Guide To Building Community Around Your Blog. Retrieved October 01, 2020, from https://www.quicksprout.com/building-community-around-your-blog/

Hennessy, B. (2018). Influencer: Building your personal brand in the age of social media. New York, NY: Citadel Press, Kensington Publishing.

Gillian, P. (Producer). (2019, August 13). How to Make Money with a SMALL Audience (ft. Pat Flynn) [Video file]. Retrieved September 12, 2019, from https://www.youtube.com/watch?v=y8qflFrVPMo

Patel, N. (Director). (2019, January 31). 7 Social Media Hacks That'll Make Your Business Grow Faster | Neil Patel[Video file]. Retrieved from https://www.youtube.com/watch?v=3x9AWh7g1YQ

Scott, J. (2019, December 19). How to Increase Instagram Engagement With Stories in 2020. Retrieved March 07, 2020, from https://www.jeffbullas.com/how-to-increase-instagram-engagement/

Kelly, N. (2012, March 23). 5 Tips for Moving Social Media Leads Into the Sales Funnel. Retrieved July 07, 2019, from https://www.socialmediaexaminer.com/5-tips-for-moving-social-media-leads-into-the-sales-funnel/

Kelly, N. (2011, July 20). 6 Ways to Convert Social Media Traffic Into Leads : Social ... Retrieved September 1, 2019, from https://www.socialmediaexaminer.com/6-ways-to-convert-social-media-traffic-into-leads/

John. (2018, June 20). Social Media: How To Turn Followers Into Customers. Retrieved March 07, 2020, from https://plumdirectmarketing.com/blog/social-media-leads/

Elsbury, K. (2019, August 19). Council Post: Four Ways To Brand Your Company On Social Media. Retrieved September 01, 2019, from https://www.forbes.com/sites/theyec/2019/08/19/four-ways-to-brand-your-company-on-social-media/

James, M. (2019, September 17). How to Create the Perfect Facebook Ad in 10 Minutes. Retrieved September 07, 2019, from https://blog.hootsuite.com/perfect-ad-facebook-minutes/

Barnhart, B. (2019, October 09). 9 Smart Social Media Tactics You Need Today. Retrieved October 10, 2019, from https://sproutsocial.com/insights/social-media-tactics/

Patel, S. (2016, June 27). 8 Ways Podcasters Can Profit From Their Shows. Retrieved October 09, 2020, from https://www.entrepreneur.com/article/277912
ABC News (Producer). (2018, November 28). What is TikTok? | ABC News [Video file]. Retrieved January 1, 2020, from https://www.youtube.com/watch?v=mQEGJMmqBTw

An Inspirational Word
from the Author

What Does It Really Mean to Shine?

Capitative
Illuminate
Show   Up
Show Out

OR

Creating Your Destiney

Shining is a multi-faced adverb. It does not elude to just one thing and it does not exclusively apply to any one person. Each individual is gifted and skilled in different areas. Therefore, each in- dividual has the ability to shine in their own way. The word shining is defined by Merriam-Webster's dictionary as possessing a distin- guished quality. Yet, we often think, oh well that person is "shiner", or a shining unique individual, that has more of a chance to stand out or shine more than we ourselves do. Then you tell yourself, I don't have what it takes. Yet you fail to see that you too are capable of shining in some way. Perhaps it's not the way that other people shine, whom you are comparing yourself to. Yet, if you were to look at your own unique gifts and how you can use them, you wouldn't feel any less than the other person who they think is more of a shi- ning success than you are.

For example: You have a friend that's a great soul singer. She singers her heart out at a talent showcase and the crowd goes wild, clearly, she's shining. You are a visual artist with talent in painting. By the age of 24, you've painted hundreds of pieces, yet no one has yet to see your work and deep down you feel like you'll never get the recognition that you desire or deserve. Well, sorry to say this friend, but it's all in your mind. The only reason you aren't shining-- is you. Yes, you, because your limited mindset won't allow you to see or feel like you are winning or shining. So, you are not.

You shine when you are able to captivate an audience for an intended or unintended purpose. You truly start to shine, when you shine from within by truly loving yourself and enjoying what you do best. If you want to shine, believe you can. First, honor your gifts and appreciate what you uniquely have to offer. Next, find ways to share your gift with the world. Make the world your stage, and sing like a caged bird freed, by showing your talents in innovate ways. Remember It's your time to shine, so shine on em'.

This book is one great tool that you can use to shine via building your brand in epic ways on social media. My ultimate hope is that it helps you to not only build your brand online, but to have faith in it and start to radiate- shine.

Follow more inspiration from Sunshine West check out her blog www.SunshineWest.org and Instagram @Sunshine_West_Ceo.

About Learn Media Today

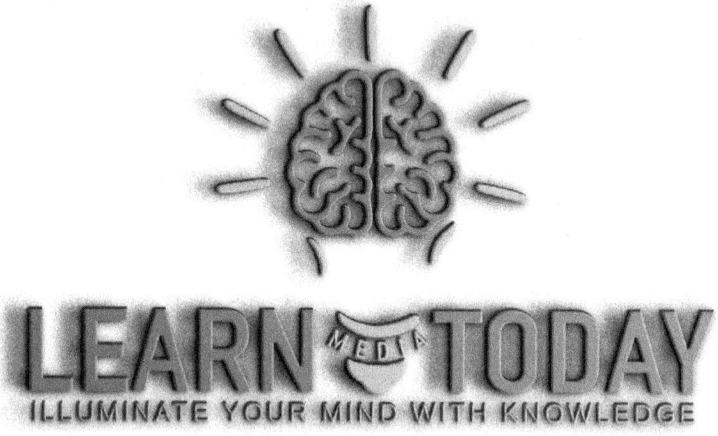

Learn Media Today is a training business that helps other businesses to grow their brands and all people to grow their careers by providing solutions that include online media training, coaching, online tools and marketing services.

Learn Media Today provides training and services in the areas of:

ï   Social Media Marketing

ï   Media Production

ï   On-camera Performance & Speaking

ï   Career Development & Resume Review

ï   Business Branding

To find out more about how we can serve your brand reaching out on www.LearnMediaToday.com or my coaching website www. SunshineWest.org.

For assistance with brand creation, social media marketing and brand design contact us at www.SunshineWest.org or www.Learn-MediaToday.com or email us.

Connect with Our Social Media Community!

Connect with us online for free training tools, inspiration and deals especially for followers on Instagram @LearnMediaToday and @ShineOnline.Book.

More About the Author

How did I Get the Name Sunshine?

I've always been ok with shining and being the live-outload, sunshine, in the family. My mother often recalls my inner shining confidence that I displayed as a very young child. I think my confidence has always been inherit, sort of build in and a bit surprising to some—but not to dad. Dad always knew his little girl would be something special, "Sunshine" he says, "Remember you are Sunshine". Why? I ask. — "Because you were born in the sunshine he says". He then interprets that as I can bring this "Sunshine" where- ver I go. That powerful statement stayed with me. That's where I got the name Sunshine.

Here we see that confidence starts at home, with parents love and encouragement. Yet no matter how much parents try to pre- pare you for the world—some things you just learn the through experience. These experiences become the real test of your faith, in your God and in yourself. For me I think seeing true faith come to fruition began when I made it to the Tyler Perry's Madea Family Reunion movie set at age 19, something I thought could only happen in my wildest dreams….and it did. Yet, many lessons came before that, would lead me there and carry me forward to entrepreneurship.

Follow my journey on Instagram @Sunshine_West_CEO

Thank you for reading!
-Sunshine West, CEO

Where Can You Find Information About Training and Coaching?

You can find media training in the areas of media production, acting business, on-camera performance, career development, business branding, social media marketing by reaching out on www.LearnMediaToday.com and www.SunshineWest.org. For assistance with brand creation and design contact us at www.SunshineWest.org or www.LearnMediaToday.com or email us.

Connect with us online for free training, inspiration and deals especially for followers on Instagram @LearnMediaToday and @ ShineOnline.Book.

Connect with our media production company for event photography, educational films, media& film production, mediamarketing strategy and promotional videos/Ads at www.20WestEntertainment.com and follow us @20WestEntertainment

Acknowledgements

Thank you to everyone that has encouraged me in my business and career.

Thank you, mom for supporting all of my endeavors and the rides you provided for auditions when I started acting for film. Thank mom, for being my first fashion stylist and biggest supporter.

Thank you, dad for teaching me the importance of business and being a model business owner.

Thank you, sister, Ro, for always being a support system and friend. Thank you for coming to my first business grand and helping me to shine and see my ability to be a star. Thank you, sis, for encouraging me to write my book.

Thank you, little brother for being our family's "tech guru" and gaming expert.

Thank you to my book graphic and logo designers.

Thank you to my book editors.

Thank you to my book launch team. Without your support I could not make it.

Thank you to the City of Atlanta, GA for the endless opportunities provided for artists, creatives and female business owners like myself.

Thank you to my graduating universities Georgia State University and Southern New Hampshire University.

Thank you to my city of birth, New Orleans, LA, for the amazing cultural influence that has led me to becoming an artist and influencer in my community.

Last but not least, thank you to all my family in New Orleans, LA and the ancestors who taught us to pray, have faith and tell our stories.